Psychic
Communication
with Animals *for*
Health *and* Healing

Psychic
Communication
with Animals *for*
Health *and* Healing

Laila del Monte

Translated by Jon E. Graham

Bear & Company
Rochester, Vermont • Toronto, Canada

Bear & Company
One Park Street
Rochester, Vermont 05767
www.BearandCompanyBooks.com

Bear & Company is a division of Inner Traditions International

Originally published in French under the title *Communiquer avec les animaux* by
Éditions Véga, 19, rue Saint-Severin, 75005 Paris
First U.S. edition published in 2010 by Bear & Company

Library of Congress Cataloging-in-Publication Data
Del Monte, Laila.
  [Communiquer avec les animaux. English]
  Psychic communication with animals for health and healing / Laila del Monte ;
translated by Jon E. Graham. — 1st U.S. ed.
      p. cm.
  Includes index.
  ISBN 978-1-59143-100-8 (pbk.)
  1. Extrasensory perception in animals. 2. Pets—Therapeutic use. 3. Animals—
Therapeutic use. 4. Animal intelligence. 5. Perception in animals. 6. Human-
animal communication. 7. Human-animal relationships. I. Title.
  QL785.3.D45 2010
  133.8—dc22

                                                                2009050670

Printed and bound in the United States by Lake Book Manufacturing

10 9 8 7 6 5 4 3 2 1

Text design by Jon Desautels and layout by Priscilla Baker
This book was typeset in Garamond Premier Pro with Cochin used as the display
typeface

To send correspondence to the author of this book, mail a first-class letter to the
author c/o Inner Traditions • Bear & Company, One Park Street, Rochester, VT
05767, and we will forward the communication.

Contents

Foreword by Michel Robert ... ix

Foreword by Patrizio Allori "Hevatan" ... xi

Preface ... xiii

1 ✦ The Wolf ... 1

2 ✦ Formentera ... 7

3 ✦ Telepathic Communication ... 13

4 ✦ The Simple Communications ... 21

5 ✦ Animals and Their Hearts ... 34

6 ✦ Animals and Their Bodies ... 56

7 ✦ Unique or Strange Cases ... 72

8 ✦ The Messenger Birds ... 79

9 ✦ The Primordial Language ... 86

10 ✦ We Are Not Alone ... 89

11 ✦ The Signs   95

12 ✦ The Awakening   99

13 ✦ When They Come into Our Lives . . .   105

14 ✦ They Are Our Teachers   109

15 ✦ Cat Gurus   120

16 ✦ They Explain Who We Are   127

17 ✦ How to Forgive   135

18 ✦ Lessons   145

19 ✦ To Love   150

20 ✦ When We Think We Have Been Parted   156

21 ✦ The Doorways   162

22 ✦ Preparation   167

23 ✦ The Afterlife   172

24 ✦ When You Light a Candle   179

25 ✦ Light   191

Index   202

From the bottom of my heart, I thank the wonderful people I met in Europe for the beautiful, deep friendship we now share. I also thank them for the love, help, and support they have so generously provided me. Finally, I thank all those who have contributed to the final realization of this book.

Foreword

Michel Robert

Former member of the
French Olympic Equestrian team

When I first heard of Laila during a horse competition, I immediately wanted to meet her. A short time later she came to see me at the stables.

That day my horses had arrived by truck from the Gijon horse show in Spain. One of them had suffered an attack of claustrophobia just before arrival and, while struggling to escape, had fractured and displaced his lower jaw. When I saw his bleeding mouth and that severe displacement due to the fracture, I thought that we could care for him ourselves, but how?

On the day of the accident, by chance Laila had come with a horse dentist. Together with Laila and with our hands placed around the fracture, we transferred energy to the horse four times, forty minutes each time. Little by little, and without any other outside intervention, we saw the fractured part, which was hanging loose, move until it was completely back in place. So strongly did we believe in this cure while we administered it that it actually took place.

The next day the horse was in good shape, and three days later he was eating normally, with no negative effects for his jaw.

I believe more strongly than ever that with horses, if we are truly present, aware of our sensations and intuition, and able to use our natural faculties, it is possible to know, to cure, and to communicate. Of course, we must detach ourselves from all our prejudices and negative habits. Laila has so much experience and so much feeling that her communication is successfully transmitted. Her faith and tenacity allow her to occupy an important position and to be recognized even in a world of skeptics.

With regard to myself, for the past few years I have been aware of the reality of communicating with animals in order to sense their desires, their ills, and their reason for being, and I believe that in the future we will be able to know more and more about them, thanks to animal communication.

Foreword

Patrizio Allori "Hevatan"

Horseman of Italian Cheyenne descent

I am merely a horseman, but I belong to a culture that is thousands of years old. In traditional medicine ceremonies I have witnessed exceptional things. My meeting with Laila is one of these extraordinary experiences. I was quite skeptical initially when several riders from the French jump school and a mutual friend told me about her. What convinced me—or perhaps a better way to put it, what instinctively inspired my interest—were her simple human qualities. The medicine men or those leading the Cheyenne ceremonies are among the simplest and most humble people I know. It seemed to me that Laila possessed these same qualities. I understood that the spirits had chosen her and that this could very well have turned out to be an excellent choice.

Insofar as I am only a horseman, a traditional trainer, I spoke with several elders at the reservation (Lame Deer, Montana) about her. I received the confirmation I had expected, and the second workshop was to allow for a meeting between Laila and several respected medicine men. I therefore invited her to join me in Montana during the summer. We had spoken with a Sun Dance priest by the name of Mark Wandering Medicine. Confirmation of her potential direct contact with the spirits was not long in coming: immediately on entering his presence, we noted that Laila received exceptional and concrete information pertaining to him. Mark showed great respect both to her and to her connection to the world outside space and time. He was surprised and almost overwhelmed by this "young" woman.

I tried to understand what Laila explained and taught during the workshops, and it all formed part of the Amerindian culture. Confirmation of this was provided by all the elders of my people with whom I had spoken. Because of this I was happy to combine our experiments when Laila and I gave workshops together. Laila's communication and the Amerindian way are two different routes to achieving the connection that forms part of the same philosophy and the same culture—or better, the same way of life.

Laila is not an advertising or marketing expert who makes use of the latest techniques in today's world of horses and equitation. The truth within her, her sincerity toward herself, her devotion to what she does, and the respect to follow in the present day a path carved by Amerindian experience has caused her to become an integral part and expression of this people. In my opinion Laila is not a new guru with exceptional intellectual gifts who is immersed in publicity campaigns with economic interest being her top priority. The continuous work she does with the aid of medicine men is a guarantee for me, a guarantee for anyone learning from her, and a guarantee for all to be protected by the experience gathered in thousands of years of Amerindian culture—an indigenous cultural expression that claims relational experiences with nature based on an ecological balance that we call the sacred circle of life. Because of her innate sincerity, it is inside this circle that I place the work performed by Laila.

Preface

This book is a description of my personal experiences. I therefore invite you to take whatever you find in it that echoes within your own heart.

It is important to respect the true nature of an animal. We should never confuse any animal with a human being, because too many of these situations are prejudicial to animals.

To be an animal communicator, it is essential continuously to perform work upon yourself. It is dangerous to project on animals your unregulated emotions and to project them on the people to whom you transmit the information you have learned. Every word has its consequences.

The purpose of a communication is not to judge or criticize a *guardian* (I use this word instead of *owner* because I feel that animals do not belong to us), but honestly to help the animal or person. When I mention that animals absorb emotions or difficulties for people, I take pains to emphasize that they do so unconsciously. A communicator should not feel guilty or criticize the guardians or people responsible for the animal.

Where does the information I collect during these communications come from? I go through the Creator, Great Spirit, and ask him to establish a communication that will allow for more precise information to emerge. The communication depends on a number of factors: the Creator is above everything, but it is up to us to do the necessary work upon ourselves. This is where the concept of free will steps in. In a communication it is our responsibility to project our mind with integrity toward the mind of the animal. The animal must also wish to establish this connection with us. It is up to us to work in a disciplined way to develop the fitness of all our senses.

How should the information gleaned be passed on to others? I would like to emphasize that whatever is seen, felt, and heard in the communication necessarily requires discernment and scrupulousness before the information is passed on. In addition, our beliefs and our emotional projections can scramble or blur the information we have perceived. The fact that we asked the Creator for the communication does not guarantee answers that are free of erroneous interpretations and projections. For each and every communication we should stick to concrete information and not venture into abstract interpretations reinforced by increasingly widespread fads in "personal development."

Next, there is the snare of the ego: We are all very satisfied when we obtain results as a consequence of these communications. The danger would be to feel superior and special in comparison to others. You really should always ask yourself: "Is this piece of information helpful and beneficial for the animal and the person?"

Finally, if I say, "Your horse says . . . ," it is an absolute assertion. It decrees that what is said is the sole truth—an undesirable situation. If I say, however, "When I communicate with your horse . . ." the choice is left to the individual person to accept or reject the information, to find it within or not.

1

The Wolf

*The Divine is present in everyone, in all beings, in every-
thing. Like space it is everywhere, all pervading, all powerful, all knowing. The Divine is the principle of Life, the
inner light of consciousness, and pure bliss. It is our very
own Self.*

AMMA, MATA AMRITANANDAMAYI DEVI

Summer 2002. I was in Yellowstone, a magnificent natural reserve and
park in Wyoming. I was there with some friends, and we had decided
to take a car to visit the park. There were four of us: David; his friend
Cathy, who drove; Conrad, a young, twenty-one-year-old man; and me.
Situated on an ancient volcanic caldera, Yellowstone is one of the most
beautiful spots on the American continent.

Our drive was truly magnificent: cascades of light; geysers gushing
out of the earth; an omnipresent odor of sulfur; the silvery ground sparkling everywhere with salts and crystals; the hot springs; the wisps of
smoke and gas; the water boiling in the ground that released a strange,
hot vapor; the violet mountains of the great canyons behind me. I found
myself in an enchanted land lost in time that was so beautiful it took
my breath away. Through the trees we could spot enormous buffalo,

elk, and deer, all watching us suspiciously. A whole population of wild animals lived on this American soil.

I especially wanted to see a wolf. I have always loved wolves. Of course, the wolves that fascinated me were those of *The Jungle Book* as well as the legendary she-wolf who founded Rome. I would imagine that she had adopted my twin brother and me and had protected us. This had nothing to do with the real world, but that did not matter to me: my dreams were more beautiful because of it.

Several years earlier, when I was in the United States, I had met a woman shaman of Amerindian and Asiatic origin. While listening to the extremely rhythmic beating of her drum with my eyes closed, the animal that appeared to me during this rhythmic journeying was a wolf. I did not know if this apparition was real or simply the fruit of my imagination. I could not put out of my mind the wolf's yellow gaze or the odor of her thick pelt to which I had clung. Now, during this visit, I wanted to see a real wolf. I had been told that Yellowstone National Park was trying to reintroduce wolves into the area after they had been wiped out by hunting. There were very few remaining, and they remained hidden.

A herd of elk approached us. A large male stood very close to us at the entrance of the bridge. He seemed furious. Three other, smaller elks, who were probably female, waited for him on the middle of the bridge. He was obviously the leader of the herd. There was no other way to get across to the other side of the river. We were quite impressed and scared. After deliberation, I was chosen to go to him as a spokesperson. My belly rumbled with fear. This elk was rather threatening with his huge antlers, and he did not at all look as though he had any desire to make way for these weak, civilized humans who were so out of place in his natural world. This was his territory, and this sparkling, deep-blue river belonged to him.

I stood at a distance that I felt was safe, and I rapidly communicated with him mentally that we would not bother him and to allow us to pass through. Nevertheless, he was truly furious and had no intention of cooperating. I explained to him that we wanted to go to the other side of the bridge. I truly understood that he did not appreciate two-legged tourists invading his territory, but I communicated to him that we did not wish him any harm. All we wanted to do was to cross this bridge. Several times I sent him images of our group walking quickly over the bridge with a kind attitude toward him. I showed him an image of the bridge, now free of these burdensome strangers who vanished into the blue-violet horizon of the mountains. After several attempts, we reached an agreement. I said to my still-nervous friends: "Now we are going to cross one by one in silence, especially making sure not to look him in the eyes." This was the day when I became truly convinced of the reality of telepathic communication; this was a test. Our friend David stepped forward courageously, and the elk allowed him to pass. David practically had to brush past him while the elk continued watching us with a ferocious gaze. I was ready to jump into the river, just in case. . . . The other elks let us pass without making a single movement.

At the end of this extraordinary afternoon we took the road back. I was dozing. David woke me up with a nudge of his elbow and said, "Look at the wolf!" I saw only a silvery shadow and the yellow sparks of his eyes as he fled from the headlights of our car. I shouted out: "Oh no, that's not enough! I really want to see a wolf!" I then immediately fell back asleep, worn out by the day's adventures.

The next day the same group of us set off on a new expedition. We planned to finish the evening on one of the purple mountains that we could see in the distance. On our return, close to midnight, we had stopped to look at the map, because we had taken a wrong turn somewhere. The fantastical and supernatural landscape in which we found ourselves was lit only by moonlight. In the air floated the ever-present heavy and intoxicating aroma of mineral salts. At the time the car was stopped, I could feel everything moving around me. I thought, "It must be an earthquake!" but my companions in the car showed no signs of anxiety. They were still concerned only with finding the right road.

All at once I felt myself leaving my body. A vast inner emptiness gave me the impression that I would never return; I was scared that I would not be able to come back. I then felt a great presence of light, a very powerful sensation of a radiant current that entered through my skull and descended along my spinal column. It was so strong that I could hardly breathe, and it seemed that it was going to make me vomit. My friend David tried to calm me, but I was barely able to contain this great force in my body. It was so powerful that it felt as though it would consume me entirely. Apparently Conrad could see what I was not capable of seeing, and he told me: "Let yourself go, don't fight it, it will be much easier if you don't resist."

I let go with great difficulty. I felt as though a round, pink, tangible light had entered through my forehead, then I was flooded with a sensation of an absolute and marvelous peace. The force was still there, but I could feel myself slipping into a timeless space that was as sweet as honey, yet dark and luminous at the same time. I had become part of the whole. It was very simple. I was nothing and everything simultaneously. I had always been in this peace without substance. Forever. It was so limpid, as if nothing else existed or was of any importance. I could no longer feel myself breathing, yet I was alive—more alive than I had ever been before. I was at the heart of this infinite, boundless space, yet at the same time I was aware of the people present in the car, the road, the forest, and the moon. I was aware of my entire life spent on this planet and aware of all the others in my life. I was part of all of them and at the same time I was absent, far from feeling any emotion, solely at peace.

I then heard Conrad's clear voice: "Now you should return. Come back!"—but I had no intention whatsoever of coming back. It was perfect where I now found myself. I knew that my body was seated in that car, but I was far away from all of that. Conrad insisted: "Come back now." Without having any intention of returning, all at once, I found myself in the seat of the car with the sensation of a powerful light in my entire back and an almost intolerable electric energy in my hands. I was completely dazed. My companions just looked at me.

I was hungry—extremely hungry. It was impossible to move my hands. Someone put a piece of banana in my mouth. It tasted strange, as if I were tasting a new variety or as if I had never eaten a banana before. I could barely control the energy coursing through my body. I heard the noise of the engine. We were going back on the road. Despite all this, I said out loud: "All the same, I still want to see a wolf!"

It was past midnight. We were in the middle of the forest, and the moon was casting a fantastic glow against the dark sky, but the enchantment was all inside my being. The forest and the moon revealed another reality. All at once, Cathy, our driver, put her foot on the brakes and said, "There's a wolf."

In the middle of the night, in the middle of the wilderness, the yellow sparkling eyes of the wolf were riveted to mine. A thin, silvery gray wolf with his ribs showing, stood all alone, just six feet away from me on the left. I could no longer breathe. I could not move my hands, which were palms up to the sky and vibrating from all the energy I was holding inside. The wolf was me, inside me, I was lost inside the gold, dark interior of his eyes. He looked at me. From time to time, he lowered his head as if eating something, but there was nothing lying there on the cold, black asphalt of the road. Then he looked at me again. Suddenly, he moved silently around the car to approach my window. At that moment, I felt a sharp twinge in my heart. The animal quickly returned to the other side of the car and continued staring at me. We were the only ones present: him and me. My companions were watching him. I could hear them breathing nearby, but it was as if they were in another world. I was enveloped by the unique and savage gleam of his eyes. I formed part of him. Everything at this time seemed extremely clear and defined, as if I had been in a fog and someone had suddenly given me a pair of glasses. Somewhere in the depths of my consciousness, I knew that this wolf was a privileged offering.

A beam of light lit up the road behind us. Another car was approaching, and Cathy started the engine again. I could feel the gaze of the wolf on my back. Ten minutes had gone by since this encounter between the wolf and me. I knew that my life was changed forever. That night I had to sleep in all my clothes in my hotel room because the energy was so strong inside my hands that I could hardly budge them. I dreamed that a pack of wolves entered my room and formed a circle around my bed to watch over my slumber.

2

Formentera

For all things share the same breath—the beast, the tree, the man . . . the air shares its spirit with all the life it supports.

TED PERRY, FROM THE FILM *HOME*

When I was little, I wanted to be like King Solomon and be able to talk with the plants, the animals, and even the stones. This was what fascinated me. At that time wisdom held no interest for me. Wisdom was for men with long beards.

We all spent our summers on the isle of Formentera in the Balearic Islands. Three months of contentment, light, and the Mediterranean. My brother and I lived at the house of Manuela, an island peasant, while my parents, who were writers, dedicated a large portion of their time to their craft. During the early years we slept in a storeroom on mattresses made from seaweed. On a rope hung from the ceiling, tomatoes had been tied to dry. It was not very comfortable, but it smelled like the sea. Later we were relocated to a downstairs room. We fell asleep to the scent of the grapes fermenting in large, ceramic washtubs.

There were very few inhabitants on the island, only one taxi—*el número uno*—a bus, and that was all. The few families who made this island their home spoke *payés,* a dialect derived from Catalan, and a little Castilian Spanish. Every Saturday we went to the village with Manuela's daughter, Carmen, to the only outdoor cinema on the island. To see the film, you had to wait for darkness to fall. The nights were extremely hot. While waiting, the inhabitants of the village strolled dressed in their best Sunday clothes. The girls walked arm in arm while their carefully ironed skirts swirled about as they watched the boys from the corners of their eyes. The boys showed off their muscles, said stupid things, and talked loudly in order to draw attention to themselves. The women sat outside, telling stories and fluttering their fans while each of the men downed a glass of wine at the café or watched a soccer match.

This was before the arrival of hippies on the island. All the films were American dubbed in Spanish but were so heavily censored that we could not understand them at all. We couldn't hear them either. Everyone talked during the film, munching *pipas* (sunflower seeds) and *kikos* (grilled corn). The boys took advantage of the darkness to caress the girls' legs secretly, or each of them simply tried to catch a girl's eye. A girl never went out alone. She was always accompanied by a *tía,* a woman wearing a black dress and the island's distinctive straw hat. As for me, I was always with my brother. We were foreigners.

The rest of our time on the island was spent on the farm. There were goats, sheep, a donkey named Ara, pigs, rabbits, and chickens. There was no electricity or running water. The toilets were outside. We used water from the well for washing ourselves. The clear water from the cistern served as drinking water for both animals and humans. Water was extremely precious, because it rained very little. If a lizard fell into the cistern and rotted inside, then the cistern had to be emptied and whitewashed with quicklime, and new water had to be trucked in from another island. There was no grass. The island was so dry that the goats ate the leaves of the barbary fig trees. I wondered why they did not prick their mouths on them. They adored them. For them these leaves were a delicious treat, like the pistachio or lemon ice cream that we loved—a delight!

Manuela showed me how to milk the goats. This was not easy. They did not appreciate my inexperienced hand. This milk was used to make the only goat cheese on the island. In anticipation of the coming winter, each cheese would be dried above the patio until it gained a certain consistency. The island's inhabitants prepared for winter long in advance of its arrival. We hunted for figs that would be dried on grape leaves. We stuffed the figs with fennel seeds that had been harvested from the sides of the road. We also dried almonds and prepared jars of olives. When September came my brother and I helped with the grape harvest from time to time. All the harvested grapes were emptied into the winepress. Carmen, my brother, and I trampled them with our bare feet. We danced and sang while stepping on the sweet, velvety flesh of the grapes, and a scarlet, aromatic juice flowed into the tub. Women were not allowed to make wine because supposedly they caused it to "turn." So, with our little children's feet, we made the wine. Nevertheless, to me it was still sour. The men, however, had a small bottle with a long spout called a *porrón,* and they threw back their heads and let the wine flow down their throats with their eyes half closed. This was the best way to do it.

We were fed on goats' milk. Manuela cut off a branch of the fig tree and opened it with a knife, and a strange, sticky, green sap flowed from it. She put it on a plate full of steaming hot goat cheese. The milk would curdle, and once the mixture was covered with sugar, it made a delicious dessert. Even the flan was made with goats' milk. One day, someone imported a cow onto the island—the one and only cow. Everyone wanted to see her, because no one there had ever seen a cow before! Later, a bull was brought in, which lived in the neighboring field. When we clambered over the stone wall to go to the "bathroom," we had to pay close attention to avoid becoming his targets.

My brother and I spent much of our time with the animals. I knew they possessed levels of perception that human beings did not have. All it took was going inside the mind of the animal. I sat on the stone wall with my brother, and we watched the goats and sheep. My brother had given names to each of them: Sa Majesté, Madame la Duchesse, Madame la Comtesse, and so on. I knew exactly how each of them was feeling on any given day: the oppressive heat, the soothing sensation of shadow, the entire herd gathered around the sole tree in the arid field, the thirst they were suffering from, the rope that made them limp—one cutting into their hooves so that they would not get out. I felt their perceptions concerning us. I had only to sit on the wall, think of nothing, and look at them, and I could capture what each of them—Sa Majesté, Madame la Duchesse, and the others—was feeling.

I also talked to the pigs. I loved to feed them leftover food. They took no offense when I teased them by spilling melon rinds over their heads. I observed that they had very quick and alert minds. They prompted a sharp sensation in my head, which I found amusing. Pigs are extremely intelligent. They appreciated my visits, especially if I had watermelon.

I also visited Ara, the only donkey of the family, who was locked up almost all day in the dark *casita* (small shed) behind the house. Always sad and exhausted, he was terribly bored. In truth, his solitude went well beyond mere boredom: he was depressed. Sometimes, when I went to see him, he turned his back on me, but I stayed next to him all the same, because he felt my presence. We remained together in silence, feeling each other there. It did him good to know I understood his situation even if I could do nothing to improve it.

I spent hours watching the ants and teasing the beetles that I found on the sandy paths. I amused myself by laying down twigs as obstacles to their travels. In the beginning they were resigned to their heavy fate, and they tried to cross the obstacles. It was a surprise to me to see that they always tried to cross without looking for another solution. To their great amazement, when I sensed they were beginning to feel too overwhelmed, I picked them up to shorten their destined path and eliminate all obstacles. I became a magnanimous deus ex machina. I also built houses out of leaves and twigs for the snails I rescued from the road, most often with their shells cracked. I did not know if their habitat could repair itself, so it seemed necessary to make them new artificial houses. I loved the silvery trails they left on the leaves. They were relieved and grateful, but the next day, I discovered that they had abandoned the houses I built for them.

I also felt it was worthwhile to save flies from an imminent death when they fell into the laundry detergent. They were always extremely scared, and they struggled with all their might to get out. This created an electrical wave that traveled through all the fibers of my body. I then introduced to them a small piece of wood that served as a lifeboat. I enjoyed the sensation they felt when, astonished, they found themselves in the sunlight, bathed in detergent as if drunk. Their transparent wings seemed to tremble from their joy to be alive. The rest of the time I detested flies and regretted having saved their lives!

So flowed the months and the joys of living on Formentera. Because I was young I was connected to all of nature. Everything there was living, everything there breathed, and I breathed with it. Everything vibrated and formed a part of me: the sand burning beneath my feet, the aroma of the fig trees penetrating all my cells. The juice of the blackberries that flowed down my throat became alive like nectar of the gods. The white houses, painted with lime, invited me to rest and told me their memories while I waited for the coolness of the evening. Even the silence, interrupted only by the crickets beneath the oppressive noon heat, filled me with its breath—and filled all the beings, large and small, who inhabited the island.

As a young child I knew in my innermost heart that everything had a spirit and that everything permitted a dialogue. Often, at night, I slipped outside and danced for the moon; spoke to the spirits of the water well, who responded to the echo of my voice; and sat at the foot of a large pine tree to which I confided my secrets. I knew there were little beings living everywhere, hidden in nature, and that they were observing me. Sometimes, I found special places and I left offerings there of thyme and stones I had found on the seashore. I loved fairies, and I spent hours drawing them and coming up with first names for them. I often lived in an inner world, constantly renewed and wonderful, that I built entirely in my head. There were no toys on the island, so it was the island itself that became for me a giant batch of modeling clay, shaped by my imagination.

Yet growing up in Paris, I lost all this. First, it was extremely hard to dream in school. I had to come up with subtle techniques so the teacher would not catch on. In addition, once we have reached a certain age, we are no longer supposed to believe in fairies—it is even worse than believing in Santa Claus!

So I learned to be critical, to set forth theories, to judge, and to produce essays. There was no longer any place in my head to listen to nature or my inner self because my consciousness was inundated by noisy thoughts that came in waves. From time to time I rediscovered an inner presence in the form of magnificent dreams or visions, to remind me that there still existed another world parallel to that of the metro, the grayness, and the intellectual discussions in smoke-filled cafés. But little by little the reality of everyday life got the upper hand. One day, when I was in twelfth grade, I received a zero in a chemistry course, because on my exam paper I had written *fairy* acid instead of *ferric* acid. The professor was furious. She underlined it three times in red ink, followed by several exclamation points.

After I completed school I became a professional dancer, and I left Paris to live in Madrid. I had to rehearse constantly to develop my technique and to maintain my ambition to keep reaching, to be more, to become the best. I knew that there was a part of me that had been forgotten, but I had neither the time nor the energy to find it again.

3

Telepathic Communication

> *In the beginning of all things, wisdom and knowledge were*
> *with the animals, for Tirawa, the One Above, did not*
> *speak directly to man. He sent certain animals to tell men*
> *that he showed himself through the beast, and that from*
> *them, and from the stars and the sun and moon should*
> *man learn . . . all things tell of Tirawa.*
>
> EAGLE CHIEF (LETAKOS-LESA), PAWNEE

I communicate with animals, and thanks to this communication, I have been able to make the long journey to find again what I had understood when I was small. Eventually I left Spain and was living in the United States, where I was completely invested in my career as a dancer. One day I saw a small ad for a course on animal communication through telepathy. I did not expect to have any results at all. I knew all too well that I was hypersensitive, but to me this was more of an obstacle than an asset. It caused me more suffering than anything else. I was like a sponge: I felt everything, I took in everything, and—what's more—I was touchy. All these sensations could be directed against me.

In the world of flamenco and the stage, I was constantly confronted with criticism and judgment. That world made me feel I always had to be accepted in order to have value; I always had to be more than the next person. In fact, all artists want to be more than the next person, and they are often envious and critical of one another. It is strange, because to me art seems marvelous and spiritual. In the beginning this critical attitude—especially among the greatest artists—was very disconcerting to me. I could not manage to grasp why they were so critical of each other, but, after years, I have become used to it. The worst kinds of insults were used by the great artists as they passed judgment: *No sabe bailar* (He does not know how to dance) or *esta fuera de compás* (He is out of rhythm). Once such edicts had been decreed, it was as if a leaden silence—cold and hopeless—fell over the room. Later I too fell into this trap of gloom. I have seen more than one person stumble into it. It was quite a fall. I had chosen dance because to me it was joyous and light—and I had become a professional dancer whose heart was dark and full of anxiety.

I lost the innocence of my childhood. Telepathy worked more to my detriment than anything else inasmuch as all I could feel were negative thoughts. It was in this first course that I discovered that telepathy is not a weapon but a tool. I began to rediscover who I truly was. Starting from the moment I began the course, I decided to seek out complete training in this field, despite the fact that I already possessed the ability to communicate in this way. I wanted to go further, and I felt this was the right path for me to take.

So I eventually became a professional animal communicator. Such communication takes place through telepathy. When people hear the word *telepathy,* they often imagine that we enter another's head and impose our own thoughts—but this is not what it actually entails. In telepathic communication we receive the animal's impressions. They can arrive in the shape of words, images, or sensations. This is how we—people—truly communicate among ourselves, but we are accustomed to hanging on to words. Yet there is a very rich world of impressions behind words. Because animals have no vocal cords to form words and phrases, we can learn from them by looking directly for impressions.

First, I establish a communication in which I receive impressions, then I decode these impressions—translate them in some way—in order to be able to pass them on to the human being(s) who cohabit with the animal. Through communicating I can gain all kinds of information about an animal, particularly concerning his moods and emotions toward a human and toward other animals around him, and I can better comprehend his desires. As in all of us, there is a very large range of desires in animals—except that we do not realize it, because we cannot hear them.

For example: Does the animal want to enter a contest or not? Does he want to stay with this person or in that location? Does he want to continue to live if he is sick, or does he want to leave this world? Through communication it is also possible to look at an animal's physical body to see how he is feeling: whether he is generally miserable or feels pain in a particular spot. If he is sick, for instance, we can learn whether an animal is capable of running a race. Communication also makes it possible to transmit a quick message to an animal. I send such messages in images. For example, I might want to tell the animal: "Don't go out in the road, or you'll get run over!" or "There are coyotes in the neighborhood; it's dangerous. Do not wander too far." I then send images of the car and the impact of its collision with the animal or images of the coyote and his fangs. I add sounds and even odors. The more vivid and detailed the images are, the clearer the message will be. For example, in the case of the coyote, I also send the odor of his fur and breath, as well as the sensation of his teeth latching on to the throat of the prey animal. All of this makes it easier to visualize. I try to form a complete picture of the situation. Of course, this is a holographic projection into the future of something that might happen to the animal, and it in fact translates as: "If you go far from the house, you run the risk of being eaten by a coyote!" I, too, have this combination of images in my head, but it happens so quickly that I do not realize it. This is how I specify to the animal that I am not translating a reality, but a virtual possibility in an undefined future, and that he should not try to put himself in danger intentionally as a means of challenging fate.

When I look for a lost animal through communication I receive images and sensations. For example, I feel the animal's paws on the grass or cement, I feel the texture of the ground beneath his feet and whether it is windy, sunny, or snowing and whether an animal is near a field or a road. I put myself in the animal's place and look at the world through his eyes. These are the traditional methods for communicating with animals and for receiving and sending information. Yet every communicator is different, depending on which of his senses is the most highly developed. Some hear more acutely, others see acutely, and still others feel sharply. The ideal remains owning all of these senses simultaneously, which ensures that the communication is more complete.

When I make a communication I proceed in stages. In the first phase I establish contact with the Great Spirit by projecting my mind toward the Creator of everything that exists. I then meet the animal on an imaginary path that I see is in front of me. In this meeting we cannot make any distinction between the imaginary and reality. Later, with practice, we can manage to discern what is fantasy and what is real communication. Each of us requires training to gain more facility with our ability to communicate. To be certain I am talking with the right animal, I need from his guardian a photo, the animal's name and age, the name of the person with whom he lives, and the country or location where the animal is currently. I can also work without a photo—but it is much easier if I have an image of the animal at my disposal. A photo makes it possible to contact the essence of the animal. It really isn't enough to have only an animal's name, such as Sandy, because there are thousands of Sandys of all shapes and colors in the United States. Over the course of the communication I observe the animal I find in front of me. I examine his personality: Does he seem welcoming, distrustful, content, sad, energetic, tired? I stay with him, simply being in his presence. I *capture* him, as if I was actually with the animal.

When I enter a house where there is a dog, I begin by capturing the animal before I approach her. *Capturing* in this instance means receiving a set of sensations and information that comes to me in the space of about a minute. This allows me to decide whether to approach the dog. Long-distance communication works exactly the same way, but in the beginning it takes a bit longer to decode the information I receive. Next, I communicate internally with the animal, and I ask him questions. I listen to the answers that come in the form of images, perceptions, sensations, or thoughts. Most important is that I listen, tune in. As human beings, we are quite accustomed to talking constantly. It seems there is constantly a flow of words coming out of our mouths, and if anyone listens to us, it is because they are obliged to listen. When someone is talking to us, then we have a response ready, and this state of anticipation does not allow us truly to hear what someone is saying. Animals, however, listen carefully, and this is the reason why we feel understood and loved in their presence.

When I am in front of a horse, the first thing he does is to try to perceive me. All his senses are awake in order to capture my presence, my being, and who I am. He listens before communicating. I, too, once spoke very quickly, and I often interrupted others. Fortunately, in Spain, everyone talks fast—so I was no exception! It was through tuning in to animals that I learned to speak more calmly, to enter into the silence, to hear the other. I realized that it was during this time of tuning in that I was truly in the present moment—it was impossible to project myself into the future, the past, or a daydream. I had to be completely focused on the here and now. I had to be.

When I am communicating after tuning in, I feel as if I am the animal who is in front of me. By seeing the world though his eyes I cannot be mistaken. To accomplish this transference I must remove myself from all my concerns, my stormy thoughts and strong emotions. I must create a void in myself. It sometimes happens that I need to postpone the communication to a later time if I am not in a peaceful state that particular day. If I am irritated or feel as though I am going to cry, or even if I feel quite joyful, my communication can be affected. With practice, however, we can manage to find our center very quickly. This silence is always inside us, and we can gain access to it at any time.

In this state of calm, we shed all our habitual judgmental attitudes, for we can transfer these to the animal. We all have a deeply rooted belief system connected to our childhood, our culture, and our environment. It is not easy for us to take this apart or extricate ourselves from it. To do this we should become the other—we should be the other. In this way, we find a blurring of the walls that form our beliefs and our negative and positive judgments, and we are then in a position to receive all kinds of information in the form of thoughts, sensations, or images. We hear what we need to know in order to help the animal—no more and no less. Most important is the desire to help. It is advisable to do a first communication under the guidance of an individual experienced in such communication.

After I begin a communication I wait so that I can possibly receive additional information, which may come from the universe or the quantum field or whatever you feel most comfortable calling it. Sometimes it comes right away, but other times, I simply have to wait. There are many different techniques for communicating. It is important to remember that we all have the same language and this language belongs to us. We need only find it. Telepathy was the true universal language before the separation of tongues during the time of the Tower of Babel. Telepathic language is like a beautiful diamond that has long been buried in a mine. We should only scratch it a little, remove the dust, and polish it. The techniques of communicating telepathically are simply tools for reawakening the memory. It is not important to know which one we should use. Once we have been able to communicate with animals, we can then communicate with the whole of the universe, because everything has a consciousness, everything—even the stones—has a mind. In the same way that our words are received and heard in the universe, all our thoughts and all our emotions vibrate and affect other minds, other spirits. This is why we should be aware of what we say, what we feel, and what we think. Not only does a dog or cat lying at our feet understand us—although their faces never betray this comprehension—but also our horse understands when we are out riding or when we are talking on our cell phone. We are heard even by the spiders on the walls and a good many other beings above, below, and from all over the universe. We are totally surrounded!

In order to know what an animal is feeling, it is especially important for us to realize just how aware animals are. They have already mastered interspecies communication. We should remember this, awaken our consciousness, and thereby repair the disorder we have sowed on our planet.

It is important, also, to note that animals are free beings; they are not our property. They come to us on this earth and choose to share their lives with us. We cannot really buy an animal because it is impossible to own another living being. Animals form part of Creation just as we do. It is erroneous, then, to place a value on an animal. This is only logical. An animal cannot cost a hundred, a thousand, or a million dollars. Once upon a time, we used to sell girls in marriage for a couple of sheep or the entire flock or for camels, depending on the family's social status. In our present culture in the West, it would not occur to us to affix such a price on a child, because we find it an abomination that slavery or commerce based on human beings could even exist. I hope that one day the same will be true for our domestic animals. They are sent to us. It hardly matters whether they come from a pet store, a breeder, or the street. Sometimes they come straight to our door. Even in a "five-star hotel" for cats, with many customers to take care of and feed, a newcomer never arrives by chance. It will always be present for some reason—whether to help us get a better understanding of circumstances or occurrences or to teach us a large or small life lesson. The size of the animal does not reflect the size of the lesson. Our lesson has already been decided long before the animal's coming.

One day, perhaps, all of us will be able not only to communicate and collaborate with animals but also to learn from them. Though games and competitions are important to us, and we love creating such competitions and tests, complete with large prizes, it is important for us to remember that we are not an animal's master or owner. We are only the guardian. For the moment, these animals are under our supervision. We simply take care to see that they are fed, housed, and loved. If they want to leave and cannot be found again, if we have looked everywhere and they still have not come back, then we should simply let go.

We are on this planet to live in harmony with the world of animals in order to explore, together with these travel companions, the palette of the more subtle emotions. If they must leave this planet because it is time, or quite simply because they wish to visit other dimensions, we cannot cling to them. Their spirit waits for us to be ready to leave. It is a hard thing to lose the little or big furry body that we have loved so deeply, but the animal's spirit is not attached to his or her physical envelope. If all of us knew the love that the Creator or Great Spirit has for us—so vast and infinite—we would find it much easier to let them leave! Love is beyond attachment.

4

&

The Simple Communications

Give me the gift of a listening heart.

SOLOMON, I KINGS 3:9

It was asked of me to communicate with a lost iguana. I get all kinds of requests in the United States. I set off in search of Freddy. First I asked the Creator, Great Spirit, for a communication with the iguana. I was provided his name and name of the person with whom he lived, Isabel. The exact neighborhood was specified in which he lived in Los Angeles, because this is a huge city. I saw a beautiful path of white sand before my eyes and started walking down it. This path was extremely real to me; I felt the sand beneath my feet as if I was at the beach.

I met Freddy and the path blurred. Little by little I began seeing through the eyes of the iguana, I entered his body and became totally one with him while retaining my awareness as Laila: "I'm in a garden with trees, there are dry leaves scattered upon the ground. I can see only the roots of these trees, but I know that they are trees." It was as if I was looking at the roots with a magnifying glass—I could see every detail. I had never felt this with my human body. Oddly, the world seemed quite flat to me. I could not see very high, not even a speck of the sky, but I knew that it was blue. The sensation of the sun upon my body was extraordinary. It did not burn at all but instead comforted and calmed me. It was different from the light that came into my cage. The ground smelled good. It felt a little dry and crumbly beneath me, but very pleasant. Every particle of dirt emitted a different smell. I also found the air quite pleasant beneath the ground in the cool darkness of a tunnel. The soil there was darker and a bit moist and had a very powerful odor. This felt so good that it made me want to sleep there forever.

The sensations were keener than those I felt in my human body. My sense of smell was much more highly developed, and I could hear even the slightest sound. I could think quite quickly—my mind was extremely agile—and when I rested, I no longer thought about anything. There was an emptiness created around me. I did not know where I was, but I felt wonderful. I thought: "I am alive, right? What do I have to be scared of? Yes, there's Isabel, but I feel good right here and now. No, I don't think I will go back to her house. Maybe after a siesta in this cool tunnel. We shall see later . . ." By putting myself in Freddy's place, my sensations became more acute in my human body.

This is an example of what I call *simple communication,* which is sufficient for knowing what an animal is thinking. More *complex communications* are the ones in which there is a large problem that needs to be resolved: for example, emotional situations in which the animals absorb the physical problems or mysteries of people in order for these mysteries to be resolved. Often, for these situations, there is additional work that should be performed after the communication to change the animal's behavior or heal him. Here are several more examples of simple communications.

A woman called me about her dog, George, a small bulldog living in Beverly Hills. She wanted to know only if he was happy. I asked her who shared her house with her. This woman lived with her husband, their cook, and their maid. After asking the Creator, Great Spirit, for a communication with George, I saw the path open, and the dog, with a splash of white on his ear, came before me. The white splash gave him a rascally, mischievous look. He was very happy to come talk to me. George was extremely spoiled; he lived in a luxurious American mansion. He showed me several large, well-lit rooms with marble floors. I followed him from one room to the next.

George was the lord and master of this house. He went wherever he liked and did whatever he pleased—but the chef did not let him into the kitchen, yet when no one was looking, he slipped through the door whenever it was half open. He showed me the kitchen. It smelled so good in there! Sometimes he could stay there without the chef noticing. He liked this poor cook a great deal, even if the man moaned and complained all the time. From time to time, the cook would be in a good mood and would give him some small delicacies. Now, however, this man was sad because his lover was making him miserable. Several days earlier he had been weeping when he was alone in the kitchen.

Then there was the maid. According to George's description, I guessed that she was Hispanic and had just recently arrived there. She was very shy and was scared of not pleasing people. She was very nervous, and, what's more, she was a little afraid of George. She did not like it at all when he jumped up on her.

George did not worry about a thing. Today he was especially happy: he had played with his buddies, the dogs in the neighborhood. Several times a week they got together at his house with "their ladies." He was very proud of this!

Sometimes I have been called by people who want simply to transmit a message. People often ask me to forewarn their animals when they are planning to leave on a trip. One woman in Texas calls me regularly when she leaves on a journey. She asks me to warn her birds and her dog. They are much calmer following the communication, and there is less damage in the house when she returns. Animals are quite telepathic, but this does not necessarily mean that they know if and when you are going to come back. To reduce their anxiety considerably, it is often enough simply to tell them: "I will be back on such and such a date."

Fay, the little two-year-old dog of my wonderful friend Robin, had been rescued from an animal shelter in Los Feliz, a neighborhood in Los Angeles. She was a very pretty dog of average size with silky white fur. She enjoyed a very happy life with her new family, but when everyone went away on vacation she systematically did all her business on the carpet beneath the dining room table. Even if someone came by every day to feed her, her behavior didn't change: she became hysterical, barking and running ceaselessly around the house. The neighbors complained, so I asked to communicate with Fay. Once I was in front of her, I asked how she felt when she was alone. She relayed a state of pure panic! I felt its oppressive weight in her belly and the anxiety that was choking her, which caused her to jump at the slightest sound and made her extremely nervous.

When she heard someone passing by the front of the house she ran nervously to the window and started barking. She also showed me the little girl's room where she went to lie down, but Fay was incapable of resting. She rose without respite and circled through the house, which had suddenly become quite small. She also showed me images of herself when she was a pup without a mother and spent almost all her time in a cage. She wanted to sleep, but there was not enough room for her to move around. There were several children in the house where she lived when she was small. It was noisy, and she was always being picked up and pulled in every direction. She tried to get away because she wanted to sleep. I do not know how, but she managed to escape. I put myself in her place. Here, translated into my words are the sensations she felt: "I'm in the street. There's a great deal of noise. I see smoke. It's so hot out. The cement burns my feet. I'm hungry, and there's nothing to eat. I managed to drink some water from a gutter. There are rows and rows of houses. I keep walking, and I look for some cool shade in which to sleep, some grass. I try to avoid being noticed. I'm so hungry. I'm tired. I want some grass . . ."*

Fay had fears of being abandoned and being lost and alone again, without her family, without the little girl to whom she was attached. Because she did not know if they were going to come back someday, the large house was transformed into a small cage with bars. The sensations she experienced of panic, rejection, and anxiety gained the upper hand. I explained to her that the family was not going away for a long time: "They will be coming home soon, and they love you." I sent her images of her beloved family opening the door, entering the house, and picking her up in their arms. They were very happy with her welcome. I also explained to her that she should guard the house during their absence—she was no longer a puppy, and this was her job. In pictures, I showed her that her family was very proud of her because she had protected the house. Little by little, Fay calmed down. Of course, she was not terribly happy to be left all alone in the house, but she stopped going to the bathroom inside.

Sometimes, people ask me questions about their animal companions' tastes and preferences in order to know what they like or where they wish to go or what they want to do. When we speak to such animals, they also reveal their daily concerns to us.

A woman called me about her dog, Brendon. During a competition he had become very nervous when in front of the judges and started salivating and peeing. Brendon, a handsome caramel-colored dog with melancholy eyes, communicated to me that he did not wish to be in dog shows. He wanted to stay at home and live a quiet life. The shows were too much pressure for him. He was fed up with being so stressed and

---

*The words in quotation marks in this and other communications related here are a translation of the sensations I received in my own consciousness and not the "words" of the animal.

constrained! He really enjoyed doing the exercises with Marge, but the shows were something else entirely. I relived the show experience with him: "I feel my throat constrict. My legs become all weak and trembling. I hear the noise, the yells, the excitement of the other dogs. The dust burns in my eyes. I'm dragged by my leash in front of the judges. What do they want from me? I don't know what I should be doing. A warm liquid flows between my legs. Now she's going to be angry and punish me. I can't do anything else. I want to leave, but how?"

Stage fright is something I am very familiar with as a dancer, but it was even worse for Brendon because he did not like shows. He made me feel so sad. The worst part was that I did not know how to help him. All I could do was explain to Marge her dog's feelings, but she would hear none of it: "I don't understand," she told me on the telephone, "he excels at the trials, but once he appears in front of the judges, he transforms into a fearful, timid dog. It's like he is not the same animal!" I tried to help Marge understand the state Brendon was in, but she went on to say: "I understand perfectly, but he has to overcome his anxieties. He must learn. It's out of the question to stop going to shows! All my dogs are in shows—that's the reason I bring them into my home."

I do not know what happened to poor Brendon because Marge never called me back.

Sunny, a silvery-gray purebred greyhound, communicated with me on the subject of the newborn child of Nancy and Joe that had just been brought into their home. Nancy had noticed that Sunny was acting oddly around the baby. He growled whenever he was in the infant's presence. Concerned, Nancy asked me to make a communication with him. I therefore went to my white path. I liked the familiar sensation of the fine, warm sand beneath my feet. Sunny appeared all of a sudden. I had already had communications with him; he had even come to my studio for healing sessions. He was very sensitive. I liked him very much and was attached to him. He had large, limpid eyes and the delicate, sensitive head of a greyhound. He was always a little fearful. He had come from a racetrack, and, when he was no longer winning any races, he was put in a cage and was abandoned and waiting to be put down. A rescue organization picked him up.

The first time Nancy brought him to me, he had a serious skin disease accompanied by abscesses and fever. The veterinarians she had consulted could not come to an agreement on his case. It was a strange disease. They had tried everything. Sunny had approached me hesitantly on my beautiful white path. He was distrustful. I stayed a moment with him, kneeling silently next to him without asking anything. I simply was there, present for him. After a little while, he dared to look me in the eyes and felt more secure. I asked him what had happened.

He showed me his past in the races. This was a world I did not know and one I have no desire ever to know. "We are locked up. There are several of us. I'm always hungry, terribly hungry, and I'm scared. The metal noises never stop [chains, metal doors?]. There's yelling, the races, running as fast as possible. No time to rest. There's a sensation in my body of extreme nervousness, the spasms in my legs, I am unable to sleep. All the others are scared, and they cry all night, but I cannot sleep, and it has been this way for a long time. If one leaves, another comes in. When will this happen to me? Where will I go afterward? I am exhausted. I have no more strength. I no longer have any desire to live. It's all the same to me in any case, so what's the good of it? And then one day, I saw Nancy's face behind my bars, her smile, her tears. She brought me to her home. Now I feel so good: she takes care of me; she loves me. There are other animals here, three cats and another greyhound. They are calm and peaceful; they sleep all the time. They don't know what it's like to be imprisoned. In the beginning I thought that Nancy would not be coming back, that she'd left me, but now I know that she's here and she'll always return. I'm no longer hungry. Now, though, there is this baby. Nancy no longer talks to me, she no longer lets me come into her room. I'm alone and she was even scared of me the other day, as if I was going to do something bad."

Sunny "wept." Animals weep in silence, with their tears falling on the inside. I cried with him. We were both together on the white path. A large space of sorrow and solitude entered my heart. "Why has Nancy suddenly abandoned me?" I dried my tears, and I explained to him that the little, hairless "human puppy" also needed love. There was enough for everyone—but the baby was so small and very fragile, and he required a great deal of care. Later, he would grow bigger. . . . It was his turn to help Nancy. After my communication with Sunny and a little more attention on the part of Joe and Nancy, everything returned to order. Sunny calmed down and courageously accepted the presence of the little "human puppy."

Lady was a purebred, chocolate-colored water spaniel with innocent and mischievous hazel eyes and curly ears that gracefully framed her head. She lived with Joyce, a breeder and trainer. Living together were five other dogs of the same breed, and all of them were in dog shows. Lady was in training and was taking courses. She was scheduled to leave soon to stay with someone for special training. It was far away, and she would have to travel by plane. The problem was with her older sister, Noemi. This was why Joyce had called me: Lady and Noemi were at each other's throats.

Here, in my words, are the sensations I perceived in Lady: Noemi, the elder dog, had won every prize at the shows and did everything perfectly. It was really annoying, when all is said and done! In addition, Joyce always told Lady what to do and criticized her constantly, while she found Noemi perfect. "She's always watching me and scolding me. I do everything wrong! It's never good enough. I've had enough! I can't take it any more! And, what's more, to her, I'm not pretty enough: my muzzle is too wide and my body is too long. According to Joyce, Noemi is perfect. She's the one who wins all the prizes. I don't want to do these shows anymore. I'll never be beautiful enough, so why even try? I'm fed up with sitting with my head up, being obliged to hold out my paw, to hold myself nicely, to walk like this or walk like that, to being scolded and criticized. I want [translated into images] to run, play, frolic, go to the river, get dirty—very dirty and wet. I want to shake myself, and sniff around, run, act crazy, jump. I want . . . I do not want to be a Lady anymore."

I understood very well what she wanted: to be constrained no longer; not to have to observe social etiquette and obligations; not to be compelled to appear perfect, to smile, to say "good morning, Madame," "yes, Madame," "thank you, Sir," "excuse me." She wanted to be free, to run on the beach and never stop, to feel her body.

Yet she had come to earth in the form of a water spaniel, a purebred dog, born at a famous trainer's—so how much was the role of choice and how much that of fate in this dog's life? I explained to her that she was just as beautiful and perfect as her sister and that she should have confidence in herself. For the moment, she had no choice: she was a member of a family that participated in competitions, and she had been conceived for this purpose. She should at least try, and if it did not work out, then I would speak to Joyce again. On the other hand, I would ask Joyce to grant Lady more free time and to bring her to the river. In exchange, Lady would make a greater effort in her training. After communicating with Lady, I had to establish a contract between the two warring sisters, with laws, conditions, and terms that had to be respected. After all this had been put in place, you could not say that Lady and Noemi adored each other, but their spats decreased and they managed to live together without jumping down each other's throats for no reason. Lady continued to be a show dog. It appears that she now behaves like a real Lady. She has allowed herself to be tamed.

Rosie was a ginger-colored cat and Mosy was a white rabbit with red eyes, and the two fought constantly. They lived in Pasadena, a very nice city near Los Angeles. Both of them were trying to get their guardian, Cindy's, attention. Once she stepped out of the house, it was war! They jumped on each other during their endless chases and caused terrible damage in the living room. When Cindy returned home, everything was on the floor, and she would have to nurse the wounds of the two combatants. Blood flowed. In addition, during their periods of truce, Mosy would chew nervously on the very beautiful art books placed on the table, and there was all kinds of damage done to the electrical cords of the lamps, the chair bases, and other valuable objects that Mosy found succulent. When I communicated with Rosie and Mosy, each blamed the other for having begun the hostilities. Mosy even sulked. They had me running back and forth between them, which in the end became quite exhausting. I felt as if I were a Ping-Pong ball!

So I decided to take matters into my own hands. I summoned up all the diplomacy of a United Nations ambassador, and we worked on setting a date for signing a peace treaty. After much prevarication, we reached an agreement. I even made them sign a contract in the presence of other animals as invisible witnesses: a cross from the paw of the stormy rabbit and a cross from the paw of the rascally cat. I prayed to the gods that this treaty would stand. The day after this peace accord, the cat and the rabbit became inseparable friends, grooming each other and taking their naps curled up next to each other.

A mare named Charm, who lived in a beautiful, green area of northern California, told me how she had been stung in the chest by a spider during a walk. She gave me a detailed description of the man who fed her when her guardian was away. I could see him with his pail of oats: she showed me his images—he was hairy, and his cap was blue. He also wore a blue shirt. She did not like this man one bit. She never explained to me why she had this feeling, but it was quite visceral. Once he came near her, and her entire body became tense with stress. I could feel the adrenalin rising in my body and a total rejection of this man racing through me. It was strange to feel this rejection through Charm's eyes. It was more the sensation emanating from him that made her bristle. Who knows why? Perhaps she was capturing something from his past— his thoughts or actions. In any case, it made Charm—a horse who was normally gentle—into an aggressive creature. Her guardian confirmed that the horse had even tried to kick him several times. After this communication, the guardian decided to find someone else to feed the mare when she was away.

I once treated a small, black pony in a stable. He had a great deal of pain around the nape of his neck. He showed me an image of a little girl about ten years old. She had chestnut hair, and she was dressed in red. This child hurt the pony when she was mounting him: she was clumsy and pulled too hard on him as she hauled herself up on his back. Every time the little girl rode him, he suffered pain in his neck, back, and ribs. "I stretch my back to try to make sure she won't fall off and will feel more at ease, but then she holds my head too high and it pulls on me and makes my mouth hurt. She doesn't know it, though, so it's not her fault." I asked myself if I should say anything to the owners of the pony. Perhaps it was my imagination. It was also January in France, so it was quite cold. Just then, however, a young girl appeared. She was ten to twelve years old, had a ponytail of chestnut hair, and wore a red coat. She turned out to be the daughter of the stable's owner.

Night had already fallen, and though I was cold and hungry and had a great desire to sleep, I told myself it was my duty to pass along this message to help the pony—so I asked the little girl what her name was and if the pony was hers. Yes, she said. I explained to her gently that the pony was experiencing great pain in his neck and that she should be gentle with him, especially when she mounted him. I told her that humans often failed to realize just how delicate ponies are and that these horses don't complain so as not to interfere with our pleasure. I had her pass her hand over the nape of the pony's neck so she could feel it. She must have thought I was odd and must have asked herself who this lady was—but she looked as though she understood . . . I hope she did.

Children grasp things quite quickly if we take the time to explain. Not skeptical, like adults, they already know that animals communicate. Yet out of ignorance their actions can sometimes cause animals pain. I have often seen children strike their dog or cat. Even if he is their best friend and they adore him, they hit him because they think the animal is doing something "bad." Sometimes they strike to release some of their own stress from people telling them repeatedly that they are bad and are behaving improperly.

I remember a situation in the waiting room of a doctor's office in Los Angeles. A little Mexican boy was playing with his brown, smooth-haired puppy. This puppy was still very tiny and very cute, with a small, black muzzle and big brown puppy eyes full of surprise at life. The boy was yanking him in every direction and sometimes even fighting with his sister about who was going to get to hold the dog. The poor thing looked as though it was going to get drawn and quartered. They turned to their mother to complain, but she just gave them a tired glance. The boy was hitting the little puppy on the nose constantly, saying *"Malo, malo"* (Bad, bad). The Hispanic ladies in the waiting room did not say a word; at least the children were occupied. Yet my blood started to boil. I made a brief communication, but the little puppy—really extremely little—did not at all understand what was happening to him. His head was spinning, and his sole thought was finding shelter from being struck. So I explained to the little boy that animals are just like us and feel everything, just as we do. I told him that it hurt them to be hit just as much as it hurt us to be hit—and most important, you should never hit an animal.

I told him that the puppy was not *malo* at all—he was just young—and that he was in danger of becoming a big dog who would be *muy muy malo* if he was hit in that way. After a moment the child probably thought: "Who is this lady who speaks to me in Spanish with such a strange accent, and what is she talking about?" For a fraction of a moment, I saw guilt, shame, and a gleam of understanding in his eyes. He had grasped it in three seconds! Afterward, he began holding his puppy with more respect—as though the dog was a little treasure—and he would not even let his sister come near the dog. I felt a small "thank you" from the puppy when he licked my cheek. I prayed in my heart that things would stay this way.

In numerous places (the United States, Canada, France, Germany, and Spain) I have communicated with animals of every kind and color. The place does not matter, and time and space do not exist in these communications. All of them are different and sometimes distressing, but the language and emotions of animals are the same as our own. Animals experience love, sorrow, jealousy, submission, dominance, concerns, and needs that are identical to our own. Along with dogs and cats and horses, I have been asked to communicate with rabbits, a wolf, an ape, a pig, an owl, squirrels, snakes, and iguanas. They all present variations on the same theme. Words may have a different sonority in different languages, but the thoughts behind them are the same. The heart is similar everywhere, from one species to the next.

5

❧

Animals and
Their Hearts

*It is the light of consciousness that makes all valuable and
extraordinary. The little things then are no longer little.
When a person with vigilance, sensitivity, and love touches
a pebble on the seashore, this pebble becomes as precious as
a diamond. The greater your consciousness, the more depth
and meaning you shall have in your life.*

SRI RAMANA MAHARSHI

Through communication we are able to know what animals are feeling,
especially those emotions concerning their wants and needs. When I
work as a volunteer in animal shelters, I am often asked to help with
regard to adoption. By examining closely the personality and past of an
animal, I can see, for instance, if he is going to feel comfortable with a
family with children or if he requires the attentions of a single person.
I can also distinguish if cohabitation with other animals will be positive. Some animals have an extremely weighty past, and it is difficult for
them to dislodge memories of very painful traumas—just as with people
who have experienced wars or abuse. With respect to horses, communi-

cation also makes it possible to determine their physical and emotional aptitudes for competition.

I once visited a stable in eastern France. I walked in front of the stalls, with my notepad in my hand, because I had been asked there to evaluate the aptitude of these horses for competition. Initially I was very excited to do this. I love establishing communication, tuning in, standing in another's skin, searching, discovering things. All at once, however, I could see myself with my pen and paper and my know-it-all air. Behind the bars: the horses, their gaze . . . Now everything seemed sad to me, even my gaily colored shawl was drab and fell from my shoulders. I was ashamed— truly ashamed. What right did I have to come here and do this? As if I were a jury, how could I pass judgment on these animals' capabilities? I felt like a slave dealer looking at people's teeth to see if they were strong enough, tough enough for the job. My thoughts started heading into every direction while the horses just kept watching me. If they were not cut out for competition, perhaps it was better to say so—for them—to avoid any wasted time and useless training. But who was I to say whether they were cut out for it, and what if I was wrong? This was not something to be taken lightly; their whole lives depended upon it. Every word carried weight; every decision would have consequences. Whatever I did, they would still be constrained, locked up in their stalls, imprisoned. I could not give them back their freedom. I wanted so much to help them. Horses have no words to express themselves. What was I to do?

Among these horses was a twelve-year-old bay mare named Jaina, who had been trained to compete at a high level. Yet when I communicated with her, I saw that she had neither the physical endurance nor the mental disposition for this kind of work. She would have preferred to be sold to a private individual who would take care of her and take her out for rides. In addition, she really did not understand what was expected of her and was very confused.

In the same stable, the beautiful bay Naomi had great physical aptitude for competition but was somewhat scattered mentally. She adored praise. All she needed was a competent trainer, and she would perform wonders. Another horse, Leslie—despite the warts scattered over her body that drew somewhat disgusted looks—had an enormous will and endurance accompanied by a clear mind and a strong sense of loyalty. A great athletic career awaited her. She felt completely at ease in the world of competition and would navigate it without difficulty.

When I arrived at the stables I was shown a newcomer, a chestnut horse. He was visibly anxious and very nervous and would not allow anyone to touch him. Thinking that he had no desire to establish contact with me, I headed to another stall at the other end of the stables—but I had the impression that he was pulling vigorously on my shirt, so I had to take a few steps back. The horse wanted to communicate, whatever it required. I was there; I had to listen to him. Here is a translation of the sensations I received from him: "I want to stay here and not just be a temporary guest. I'm very strong and agile, I have great mental strength and a powerful will, and I want to work. Just give me a chance. I want to stay here. It's better than the other place. He [Jean-Michel, the owner of the stable] is more relaxed and has good will. The other horses seem to like him. Yet he is talking about selling me—but I really would like to stay here. I'm strong. I can do everything. I only have to show him. It seems good here . . . Especially, don't send me back to that other place. Everything is more peaceful here; the other horses are at ease."

When I explained all of this to Jean-Michel, I could tell by his expression that he was touched and that he might give this horse a chance. After this conversation I approached the chestnut horse again. He was immediately different. He lowered his head and let me touch him, his body was now completely relaxed, and he even allowed me to blow in his nostrils. In the end, he was soothed and more tranquil because someone had offered him understanding and security. He was named Lothaire and was a son of Le Tot de Semilly.*

---

*[Le Tot de Semilly was a famous jumping champion from 1988 to 1991. He was the first French horse to be sponsored by the French Equestrian Federation. His excellent jumping abilities were inherited by many of his offspring making him one of the best sires in the world. —*Ed.*]

❦

By listening carefully to what horses have to say, we can also help riders. The horse always shows me the position the rider takes on his back. Almost always there is something that does not work quite right and often gives the mount back pains. The rider often places too much of his weight forward or backward, his body leans too much to one side, he pulls too strongly on the reins, his buttocks are not balanced on the saddle, or he has a poor seat, and so forth. To restore the balance of his rider, the horse tenses his back, the nape of his neck, and even his legs. Often the horse has the sensation that his rider is going to slip or fall. This creates muscular tension that often turns into a contraction, which, over the long term, engenders other problems that often require the intervention of an osteopath.

By communicating with the horse, we can find out where the problem lies and correct it. This has nothing at all to do with the rules that we may learn in riding schools. The anatomical structure of every horse is slightly different. This is just as true of riders. It is necessary to respect the whole. Through communication we can help both parties better adapt to each other, and in this way we help riders avoid causing injuries. (Except for a few great horse riders, I have never observed a perfect riding position.) It is especially important for a rider to know that the horse never makes any judgments about a rider's skills. Through communication the animal is simply showing me images of his discomfort—which is helpful information all around.

I have found that most often lacking is the mental connection between horse and rider. When both minds merge, all the technical defects and imperfect positions take on much less importance in horsemanship. When a rider becomes as one with a horse, the animal is ready to do everything he can to support the rider. Both can perform miracles.

I made a communication with a mare who was a top-class jumper. Isis had been injured for a while, and she was not making a complete recovery. Her rider, Gérard, was thinking of selling her. By communicating with her, I discovered that she had an extraordinary temperament that was strong, loyal, and gentle and that she was endowed with a greater-than-usual mental strength and intelligence. She also had uncustomary physical capacities: extremely powerful muscles that were both supple and agile and strong, solid limbs that were fine and elegant. Her flexibility was extraordinary. She had a very rapid response time between her mind and body, which gave her a great deal of speed and fire. Even better, she had a very strong mental connection with Gérard, which enabled her to respond to what he wanted without hesitation. I compared her to a dancer at the peak of her art. When the body reacts perfectly to the artistic mind, then the technique employed by the mind becomes invisible.

Yet Isis was depressed because Gérard was talking about selling her, and she knew it. What they had done together had been her whole life; she had given her all for him. She also showed me that she had been injured during a competition when she carried another rider. It seems the position of this other rider had been unstable, and his mind had been scattered. What's more, before the jump, his seat had shifted slightly on Isis's back. Because of the mare's extreme sensitivity, she tensed into her back to adjust for this shift during the jump. Because the rider's weight was poorly distributed when Isis landed, she felt a crack in her front left knee. Despite her pain, though, she finished the trial—but she was injured. When I explained all this to Gérard, a light went on in his head and he decided against selling her. Instead, he made the necessary arrangements for her to heal completely and then started competing with her again.

Sometimes, we humans also need time to catch on.

A communication with horses allows us to understand how they feel, to save time, and to prevent them from being sold repeatedly, which causes great trauma, and as a result, they close themselves off and stop giving. It is really asking a great deal of a horse to adapt to a new location and new person. It is akin to rebuilding an entire house, starting with the first brick. Yet this kind of response is precisely what we do not see, because we have centuries of collective memory assuring us that animals do not have feelings. Gradually, though, the veil is lifting, and we are beginning to look at the world around us in a new way. Could we actually have the unmitigated pride to think that we are the only beings to feel emotion, to have feelings? Of course, we can build cathedrals and atomic bombs—but as for all the rest, we are like all other existing beings, both visible and invisible: everything around us shows a feeling that vibrates, each in accordance with its own emanation.

Claude called me about Jane's horse, Ebony. He was fearful, anxious, and unpredictable. Jane wanted to go on rides with him, but she realized that something was not right. I asked to have a communication with the horse, and I set off, walking on my imaginary path of white sand. He appeared on the horizon, a magnificent gelding with a gleaming black coat and a stripe on his forehead. He seemed to be extremely insecure and confused, and he refused to look me in the eyes. He took his time approaching me while I waited patiently, leaving it up to him whether he came to me or not. When he drew closer to me, I told him that I had come on behalf of Jane to talk to him about whatever was bothering him. I shared with him her desire to go on rides in the forest. I explained to him that this was something Jane really wanted to do. I asked him what had happened. Using images, Ebony showed me sessions in the ring with a trainer. We exchanged no words—only images and sensations. I could see the ring, the sand, and the trainer—who always had sudden mood swings. He cajoled and complimented Ebony and offered him a reward, and the horse would then approach him, but all at once, for no apparent reason, the man would become extremely angry and start insulting and hitting the horse. Ebony could not understand why, yet the traumatized and frightened animal would bravely still try to cooperate. This scenario repeated itself constantly throughout the entire session.

I deduced that the trainer either had an unstable personality or had experienced a miserable childhood or perhaps a failed marriage. For whatever reason, he took out all his frustrations on the horses. In short, he needed therapy—but that was as far as my compassion would take me. I was indignant and extremely angry at the trainer; he seemed rough and insensitive to me. Poor Ebony no longer knew which way to turn; he was confused and understood nothing. He was like a child who is constantly slapped. At present, he was unable to trust anyone. He had closed himself off entirely. Claude admitted to me that she had attended a training session and that the description was exact: the trainer behaved exactly as Ebony had depicted him. She had been shocked by it, but she did not think she could intervene, because she was no more than a novice who was still learning how to ride. Now that her feelings had been confirmed, she determined to speak to Jane about it. It was time to tell the truth and find a new location for Ebony.

We need only listen to animals to learn what is really going on. A horse can be dominant, but not strange or unstable. Before casting judgment on an animal, we should know him in his entirety. Horses have extraordinary sensitivity; they take in everything, they absorb everything. They are like large antennas. It is often up to us to fix the mistakes made by others—and we can think of this as an opportunity given to us: through acting for the good of others, we create happiness for ourselves. This is how we ourselves learn to open up.

I have often been faced with depressed animals. Sometimes it is simply due to boredom. Ennui and solitude are terrible things when an animal is living in a prison. Often a domestic animal, like a cat or dog, waits all day for his guardian to come home from work. He knows that after a certain time, they will spend the entire evening together. In nature, however, animals never get bored. Sensations of solitude, lack of interest in life, depression, and boredom do not exist, except in the event of illness.

A white cockatoo, Snow, who lived in a suburb of New York City, had gone mad. Erica called me because the bird cried in a harsh, strident tone all day, and the noise had become intolerable. She was also scared of the bird: if she went near him he became even more agitated and would peck at her aggressively. Snow was Erica's husband Steve's bird. He owned two other birds whom Erica let out of their cages several times a day. During the communication I made with the cockatoo, he showed me that he was locked in his cage all day long. I could feel all his anguish and despair from being held in a cage. I asked myself what in the world he could have done to deserve these living conditions. It was a horrible sensation. Often he was filled with a desire to explode because of how intolerable this life had become for him. Here are the sensations and images that I received through Snow.

"There is nothing to do, nothing to look at—just the same toys every day, the same wallpapered wall, the same painting of flowers, the table with the papers on it, and the window over there. I can see nothing outside of my cage. Sometimes one of the dogs walks by, but I don't care. There are three dogs, but they all avoid me. All that I have left to do is sleep. I wait for Steve. He comes home and doesn't even look at me. I squawk with all my strength, but he doesn't even hear me. He heads straight for the big black box that emits voices and music. I can't see it from here, so I squawk even louder. If I make enough noise, he comes toward me and looks in my cage. I can smell the beer on his breath. Maybe he will take me out. We can play, and all will be forgotten. Take me out! Take me out! Then when he takes me out, I climb from his fingers up to his shoulder. He smells so good. I like to nip his ear. He talks gently to me, and my heart leaps for joy.

"We rarely go into the garden. There are so many things to see there—objects of color, and sensations of all kinds. I stay with him on his shoulder, and the breeze caresses my feathers. One time everything was white outside, like the color of my feathers, and cold, wet flakes fell on me, but Steve held me between his warm hands and blew on me. This made a mist. And then he had me doing somersaults . . .

"But this time, when I squawked in my cage, Steve approached me with a bottle in his hand and told me to shut up, and then he went away. Now he never takes me out, so I squawk louder and louder. The dogs start barking. I know that my cries get on their nerves. Erica yells, and Steve shouts even louder. She cried, and now he's angry. He shakes my cage and says: 'Filthy bird, shut your beak!' He no longer loves me. He'll never love me again . . . He turns his back on me and goes into the room with her, always with her. I can't see him anymore. I can no longer hear them.

"Steve is always tired. I'm exhausted. I shut up, because it does no good to squawk. The dogs calm down. One day Erica took me out of my cage. It was the middle of the day. Steve hadn't come home, so I became furious, and I bit her. Hard. I have to share Steve with her, and to boot, he no longer spares a thought for me. I climbed on all things in the room. I let out a cry and tore the curtains and knocked down the glasses on the table. I attacked her, and she ran away from me and shut herself in her room. The dogs started barking. My feathers were lying everywhere—my beautiful white feathers were cut. I can no longer fly. I move my wings, but I can't lift myself into the air. So I clung to the curtains. After, I could hear her crying for a long time. She always cries now. I stayed where I was, not saying a thing. When Steve returned, he picked me up gently and put me back in my cage. They had a fight. I heard Steve go out, slamming the door behind him. I know he's thinking of giving me to someone else, but he's not doing it. I don't give a damn now. I'm tired."

After the communication I spoke with Erica, who asked me to explain all of this to her husband. She confided in me that he no longer had any time for her, either. After work he comes home exhausted, turns on the television, and does not talk to her. On the weekend he plays football with his college buddies. Erica told Steve that he had to take the bird out of the cage or make up his mind to sell the cockatoo. She called me again, one month later. For a week Steve had taken time to play with the cockatoo, which had been given his freedom every day and was happy. The strident cries had stopped. But after these few days, Steve had quickly fallen back into his old habits. Snow was once more in the cage. There was nothing else I could do. I had just a bit of access to the bird though communication, but I remained powerless. I can hear animals, I can understand them and suffer with them, but I cannot change their destinies.

Boredom in horses can become fatal. They are isolated in their stalls, with sometimes only an hour each day to walk outside—and not necessarily with the person of their choice. Boredom, depression, and lack of exercise are often the cause of common diseases such as osteoarthritis and behavioral disorders (for instance, cribbing and weaving). Depression always causes the immune system to weaken. For horses who are free, the story is entirely different. They live in a herd in the middle of their natural environment, and they exist inside a hierarchical structure.

It was at the Natural Riding Center of the Chateau de la Beaume that I was able to see a possibility for re-creating this environment. Sylvia, the owner, is a remarkable woman, endowed with a respect and appreciation for horses that is exemplary. The horses benefit from marvelous, green surroundings in which they live in groups and where they are free to drink from the stream and enjoy their lives peacefully as horses. They are calm and serene and do not fall ill. The horses here live in harmony, as close as possible to their true nature.

In other cases, depression is caused by the separation from or death of another animal. For horses, feeling or knowing in advance that they are going to be separated from the other horses or another animal can create a state of high anxiety. We should always keep in mind that they understand a great deal more than we imagine. They capture our thoughts.

I know a very beautiful ranch in Weiterswiller owned by my friends Ute and Lothar. It is a magnificent place located in the middle of a forest, and on the ranch, small Icelandic horses live in herds. They lead very calm and peaceful lives, and they happily cooperate to perform their work, and they respect the children who ride them every Wednesday, when they take advantage of leaving their pens to go out into the forest. Near the ring there are several box stalls that are used to house visiting horses. One day, when passing by these stalls, I saw a bay horse with a very nasty wound exactly where the saddle sat. I had already seen this horse the night before in the stable where I had stopped with a horse dentist. While there, the stable's owner showed me the saddle, an extremely heavy and uncomfortable artifact that must have dated from the Middle Ages! The poor horse looked fairly old, sad, and tired. The owner had spoken to the rider, trying to convince him to not ride the horse anymore, but he would hear none of it. He had put pomade on the wound and placed the saddle on top of it. Over the course of the day my path had crossed that of this rider several times, but I decided to keep silent. After all, I had no idea what I could do to help this horse.

Today, however, the horse was again in front of me, as if by chance— yet was this the work of fate? I examined his wound to determine how to treat it. Once I approached him, the mare in the neighboring stall became nervous and sent me thoughts: "Don't touch him." I tried to ignore her, but she projected something like a dense fog of protection around the bay horse. Would I interfere or not? My natural tendency would be to say nothing and let the situation take its own course, but this was a deep wound. If this horse continued to be ridden, it would become very serious. What's more, I had made a promise to myself to speak out on behalf of animals and to always speak the truth. I made this contract in my head, but for me it was completely real.

It is not always easy to stand in truth. It is important to be very diplomatic. To speak up without causing offense is no easy task. People are very sensitive and touchy concerning their animals— surely because the animal is often a reflection of their personality. Offending someone means you will appear in a bad light, and I do not value that at all . . . So I went in search of more information about the individuals who were riding these two horses. They were a couple from Switzerland who were trekking on horseback and had stopped at the ranch to spend the night. The woman was riding the palomino mare in the box next to the injured bay. I allowed myself to tell them politely that it would be preferable if they did not continue their trek, given that the poor bay was completely worn out and was doing quite poorly and that his wound was becoming infected.

The man, however, wanted to finish the trek all the same—for him, it was out of the question that they end it at the ranch. He had planned this ride, and everything had been scheduled in advance. One night more would spoil everything, and it was absolutely impossible to change anything. I gently insisted, with the greatest tenderness I could find inside myself. Sometimes female tenderness works. I felt that he wanted to open up to this kindness, but whenever his shell began to open, wham! It would slam shut violently: "It's out of the question! We'll continue our excursion." He seemed to be a dry man made of wood, a man whose heart was enclosed inside a carapace. His blue eyes looked at me with a cold gaze through his glasses. He was voluble, but I knew this was only a facade—like bark—and if it was removed there was a sweetness inside, pulpy white, with dew that would sometimes show and even some tears that were hidden. I then asked permission to treat his horse—who was paying attention to what was going on, just as the mare next to him.

I dressed the wound with a blend of clay and Chinese herbs that I always carried with me. While I applied the preparation, the mare was worrying about him, as if she wanted to do something. The next day the wound had almost entirely closed up, but I knew that the bay was in no condition to continue this excursion; he was still too worn out and needed rest. I explained all of this to the couple, and just at that moment I felt the mare projecting hostility toward me as if she wanted me to shut up. I was too busy talking with the couple to go see what this was all about. It was an absolute necessity for this horse to get rest. I asked to speak in private with the man I thought of as tree bark. I spoke to him about his childhood, his father, and other circumstances, and I asked him questions very delicately. He listened to me, even if he was quite distant—in fact, extremely distant inside his shell—but paying attention all the same. At the mention of his father his carapace suddenly slammed shut again, his shield went back in place, and rage overtook him. I had no further access to his interior.

There were always rules and obligations! Disappointments, cold, and a sealed heart. He was the son of a diplomat. Before leaving I placed my hand over his heart and said: "This is the only thing that matters." This was pure kitsch, perhaps, but I did not care, because it was true. I had enough of pretending. It was now or never. His eyes were moist. "I'm going to think about it," he told me. He left to take a walk alone in the forest.

That evening I saw the couple discussing something outside. I noticed that the mare was extremely agitated, and I could feel this agitation inside me though I was in Ute and Lothar's house, which was some distance from the stables. I did not want to see what the agitation was about; it upset me. That evening at dinner I learned that the couple had decided to spend another night at the ranch and to leave the next day with the mare while allowing the injured bay to stay behind. At that moment, all at once, I understood. The mare did not want to be separated from her companion. This was the reason for her agitation. How on earth had I not realized? My heart was closed, and I had not listened. I was too busy trying to convince that man. Had I done this to feel good about myself, to prove that I could convince someone, to change a destiny? Was it my ego trying to pull me to the other side, putting blinders on me? I thought: "I'll never interfere again. I won't say anything ever again." I let it be, but I could feel the mare's anguish calling me. I wrestled with myself all night, like Jacob.

The morning of the day after, the couple asked me to look at the mare, because she was refusing to eat and was acting very strangely. It was so obvious! She did not want to be separated from the other horse. They had always been together; they were bound together and supported each other. She protected him because she felt that he had less physical strength than she had. She did not know if she would ever see him again, because he was injured. She did not even know where they were, lost on this ranch in the middle of the forest. And now the riders and the horse were going to leave, abandoning him. Her entire beautiful mare's body expressed her refusal of this situation. She was not going to let the humans make this decision for her. It was simple: She was taking the first step. She was taking the initiative. By refusing to eat and not letting anyone near her, she was saying in some way: "I'm not leaving here without my companion." It was clear cut, but still I had to translate her feelings. She had summoned me the night before with her anguish and worry, and I had not listened to her. It was as if I had been wearing earplugs. She taught me loyalty, to respect my commitments, to listen. In my communication with the mare, I excused myself with the greatest sincerity. The visitors finally made the decision not to separate the two horses. They would stay several more days at the ranch until the bay was back in form. On that day a beautiful sun sparkled in all the leaves of every tree in the forest.

Animals suffer in the same way we do when we are separated from someone we hold dear. Some people never come back from mourning. They continue weeping in their heart.

When I thought my six-month-old Siamese cat Chulo was lost, Noche, my other cat, accompanied me when I went out looking for him. We knocked on the doors of all the neighboring houses. Noche stopped with me, like a dog, and listened to me asking questions. She had a magical beauty: she was a velvety night blue color with a nose like Nefertiti. She did not walk; instead, she glided silently through the world on paws of satin. She was a noble and powerful warrior, a goddess. Every morning she slipped through a half-open window that looked out over the garden, and later, with her paw, she would elegantly push through a fruit that would fall either onto my bed or onto my head. I do not know where she found these fruits—surely, in the gardens of our neighbors— but she would carry them in her mouth all the way back to the house. They were still intact! This was her morning offering. I had explained to her that I did not very much like bird remains or dismembered lizards placed in front of my bedroom door, so she opted for gifts of fruit, for which I was hugely grateful.

During our search we found out that Chulo was not lost. He would not be coming home. He had been run over by a car. The Creator had taken him from us. Never again would I feel his tender body curl around my neck, never again would I kiss his silky white belly or stare into his sea-blue eyes. His small presence, a faint light, had flown away. Finished were his frolics in the grass; finished were his adventures and siestas with Noche. Both of us adored Chulo. He was our little angel. We shared him graciously with each other. After the death of our little Siamese, there were no more fruit treats from Noche. Our hearts were broken. Noche plunged into a great sorrow from which she never fully recovered. She became weary and lost some of her beautiful fur. Noche would leave for most of the day, coming back only to eat. This was her choice. I knew she was not going far. Her absences, however, became longer and longer—but I was obliged to accept them and respect her wishes. Then one day she did not come back. I talked to her from a distance, and she showed me a woman who lived close to the house and who needed her and her presence. It was calmer there, and she would be able to forget Chulo. She sent along her love and told me not to worry, but she explained that she would not be coming back. It was time for her to move on elsewhere. I knew her new house. It was located behind my street and was surrounded by large trees. An elderly woman lived there alone, following the death of her husband. When walking in the neighborhood I had caught sight of two other cats near there. One day I stopped to say hello. I asked her if she had seen a blue-black cat. She told me that there was one who came by every day. I did not ask any more questions. It was only later in my life that I realized just how extraordinary Noche was.

We often realize later that we never love enough; we never take the time to realize the identity of the being—animal or person—next to us. We see the breath of God only after it has already passed us by.

❧

I had the opportunity to meet a goat, Miguel, who was greatly attached to a white horse. They spent the day together in a small meadow, and at night, they slept in a stall. When the horse died suddenly, the goat became sad and fell into a great depression. His life felt so empty without his companion! When a new black horse arrived, the goat was overcome with rage and frustration. He rejected the new horse completely. Their guardian told me that the black horse had bitten the goat. She could not leave them together. I closed my eyes in order to communicate with Miguel. On this occasion, rather than using a photo, Miguel was in front of me with the black horse alongside.

The goat showed me his life in images and sensations, but without any words. I could feel the pain locked in his heart. It was so strong, in fact, that I began weeping too—because it was the same pain that I had felt for all those who have left me. We always turn tears inward, even if we do understand, even if we know that life goes on after death, even if we have spoken with the spirits, even if we know that all is energy, even if we feel something is always accompanying us. We miss the physical presence of the being who has passed on, the sweet warmth of the body by our side, the sparkle in the eyes, the odor . . . It is the separation that causes us pain.

Miguel showed me his beautiful white horse, and I felt the rush of all his tenderness. The horse's spirit was large. He was magnificent. He seemed to be suspended in the air in the middle of the small stable like a resplendent holographic image. He had never abandoned his companion. He had remained near him, still together with him, enveloping him in his eternal white light. Miguel showed me the moments they had spent together, sharing them in silence—the time beneath the sun and the rain, out in the wind, and inside their stall. The time they spent together, telling each other their stories and adventures.

Here are the emotions Miguel transmitted to me, translated into my words: "I can't stand the new horse. I want him to leave. He's taking the place of my companion. Why did he leave, why? I'm alone now. The black horse? No, it was me who attacked first. After that, he bit me. No, I don't like him. I don't want him here. I will never like him. I want my companion to come back. Yes, this black horse is sad, no one likes him—but all he has to do is go away. Her? [Image of a woman] Yes, she's still crying . . . she doesn't understand either. No, that black horse, she doesn't like him either. She only has to have him taken away. It will never be the same. I don't care if that new horse is sad. I'm even unhappier than he is—I'm really hurting. I don't want anything to do with him. If he comes near me, I'll attack him again."

I opened my eyes. On the wall I saw the photo of the white horse with a woman—the blond guardian—smiling at his side. The horse had sad eyes that were dreamy and deep. I could no longer see his spirit. He could perceive the shadow in our hearts, but he did not know how to dispel it. He was powerless. Stains were already casting shadows upon the photo . . . Soon there would be nothing left. Everything disappears.

Catherine called me because her horse, Tremendo, whom she had recently acquired, refused to do anything whatsoever. Yet he had taken part in jumping competitions before. He had a great reputation and had won many prizes. She did not understand what had happened to him. I looked at his photo and went into his eyes, asking him to let me have access to him.

I was on the white path walking toward him. He approached me, sad and humble. His presence was very sweet and light. He showed me an image of a rider who was elegant, agile, and courteous. I could feel all the complicity they shared. It was a marvelous sensation. I became Tremendo: "The rider is on my back. It's comfortable with him. We leap over the obstacles together. It's an exhilarating moment; we form one entity. We win. Excited and happy, he whispers in my ear and takes care of me. Then one day, he's gone. I heard the grooms say that he was sick. Where is he? What happened to him? He isn't coming back . . .

"I waited for him every day. I waited for him a long time. Maybe he'll finally come back? I have no desire for anything. Why did he let me go? I don't understand; we were so good together. It's not the same with other people. The obstacles are not like they were, either. I've been sent to other places with other riders, but they don't interest me. I no longer desire anything. I don't care about anything. Here comes the van one more time to take me somewhere else—farther and farther from him. Now I'll never find him again. The other day on the jump course, a rider and I fell. They're going to send me away again. This is happening more and more."

Tremendo had lost all desire to sink his teeth into the joy of living; nothing interested him at all anymore. His life was directly bound to that of his former rider. Catherine knew nothing about this man—not even his identity—or anything about their history together. She had bought Tremendo, and he was now at her home, broken. This horse needed time. It was necessary to stop jumping and give him back his desire to live. Catherine was ready. "I'll keep him forever. I'll never sell him. I'll wait for him."

Tsareina, a beautiful female husky in Texas, had been found in the street and taken to an animal shelter where she was adopted by Betty, who called me to learn the cause of her dog's depression. Complicating matters, the veterinarian had also discovered that Tsareina had a tumor. She was scared of everything, she was lethargic, and she hid and refused to communicate. Yet Betty provided her with the best possible care, a house, food, and love. I spoke to Betty on the telephone. She did not know what more she could do to help her dog. I looked at the picture of Tsareina on the screen of my computer. Her eyes were empty.

When I communicated with her, she showed me images, one after the other, of the long period she had spent surviving on the streets. She had lost her family. She did not explain how to me. I saw only the street, the dust, the cars, the hunger and thirst, the injuries, never being able to stay in the same place for long because humans are dangerous, always running and never stopping, her panic, and the constant fear in the pit of her stomach. On the street it was impossible to rest; her nerves were always agitated no matter how tired she was. At present it was as if she was in a state of shock. She could not manage to find a place at Betty's and become aware of her new life. It was as if she was blind: all she could see was her past in the street.

There was not much that could be done at this point except give Tsareina time. One day she managed to escape. We spent several weeks looking for her. Betty had put up posters everywhere with Tsareina's picture on them. I made communications and tracked down her location, but no one was ever able to catch her. She was consumed with fear and would never stop anywhere more than a moment. One day she paused to drink water from a fountain in a park—she was very thirsty and wanted to stay close to the water. Someone called Betty, who made her way there, running. She called to the dog: "Tsareina, Tsareina, come!" But Tsareina took one panicked glance at her and bolted off.

Through communications I was able to follow her through the streets and parks. It was a bit like tracking from a helicopter. I knew she was dehydrated and at the end of her strength and that she would not last much longer. She no longer communicated with me; instead she fled from me as well. Finally, at the end of three weeks, someone caught her. She had not even had time to quench her thirst. They brought her to a veterinary clinic. She was worn to nothing. They called Betty, who came at once. Tsareina died in her arms, covered with tears, sweat, dried blood, and dirt. Worms spilled out of her anus; she had been eaten away from the inside. Only the Creator knows the true destiny of beings.

Promise, a ten-year-old pony, lived on a ranch in Colorado. She had been rescued a year earlier by a young woman named Crystal. Christian, who worked there as a volunteer, called me to talk about Promise. I asked what kind of work they wanted Promise to do, and whether she seemed to want to stay on the ranch. The intention was for Promise to work in the club with the children, but this pony was depressed, beaten down, fearful, and unable to trust anyone. She had been labeled as dangerous, and nobody went near her anymore. She had already caused several trainers to fall. The children of the club avoided her or made fun of her. Crystal's husband was set on selling her, and he never stinted on saying repeatedly, day after day, that Promise was worthless and that he was going to sell her if she did not behave properly.

I asked for her photo in order to communicate with the pony. She was a pretty bay with a white stripe and white stockings on her front legs. She had a noble and elegant appearance. Promise showed me images of her past and what seemed to be a very painful breaking in. I saw a man, surely the trainer, who struck her with his riding crop and abused her constantly. Her training sessions in the ring were truly torture sessions. Her mouth was extremely painful because of the bit and his overly hard handling, the saddle practically destroyed her back, and Promise's legs could no longer hold her up. She was often hungry and thirsty, but she would not give in to this man. She would not submit. I decided not to go into her body—it would be too hard to experience all that misery. I could barely even look at it from outside. She had been proud and noble; and he had broken her. He had broken her spirit! After this, she was passed from hand to hand, and there were several falls. Now she did not care at all about anything. She desired nothing, and all choices were all the same to her. This abandonment of the self is something worse than sorrow—and it is sometimes irrevocable.

After this communication I tried to explain to Christian that, first and foremost, Promise needed to recuperate physically. She required the care of a single person in order to restore her trust. This would take time. Crystal's son, Jim, was the most suitable candidate. She trusted him more than anyone else. He was calm and levelheaded. He had all the sensitivity necessary but little time because he also had his regular jobs to perform on the ranch. Christian told me it was impossible: Jim would not be able to take care of her. Promise would certainly be sold. As for the kind of work Promise wanted to do, it is impossible to talk about work to animals: this concept is foreign to them. For horses, their needs, the way they are used, and their states of mind form one complete entity.

Promise also had no idea how to answer the question about living on the ranch. All she had ever known was unhappiness and rejection, so whether she was in this place or that place—it was all the same to her. I knew that she would continue to lead an unhappy life, and I had no idea as to what I could do for her—I was totally powerless. I thought in my deepest depths: "I could help, provided she can be happy!" But I didn't put much faith in this possibility.

Five months later, Christian called me about his sick cat. In passing he told me that Promise had been placed in a shelter, where she had been adopted by a woman. As of now, Promise is living on another ranch. She seems to have regained her ability to trust, and a young girl is riding her regularly.

The key to healing a traumatized, abused animal who is totally empty and whose spirit has left, an animal with no more desire to live, is unconditional love—love without any expectation for something in return. Communication on its own is not sufficient. There has to be a person or another animal present who will mentally connect with that animal and bring her back to life. This sometimes requires time—a great deal of time—and patience.

The notion of there being a return on an investment or being profitable for their guardians causes a great deal of anxiety for horses. They do not have a very good grasp of these ideas, but they do know that if they do not please their "owners," they are going to lose their position and security and will thus be sold. The theme of selling forms part of the collective unconscious and generates huge fears. I have seen many cases of behavioral disorders simply because a guardian spoke about or thought about selling a horse while in the horse's presence. As for us, it is important for horses to know they have physical security, with food and care. Because they are not living in liberty, they are not free to roam about in search of food, and they no longer have a herd to serve as a reference point. Yet the basic necessities of survival remain identical to those in nature. The horse knows that if he does not perform well enough and does not meet the requirements of his guardian, he will lose his security. This sensation engenders anxiety, tension, and stress.

Because of this, they can explode—like pressure cookers—and are then labeled as "unmanageable." Yet in similar conditions, we humans are just as unmanageable. Love, however, melts all blockages; and patience puts everything back in its proper place. We can begin practicing this with animals. With them and through them it is easier for us to express this kind of love. We know how to do this, but some of us have simply forgotten how. Animals come into our lives to awaken our memory.

By trying to understand and help animals, the deepest parts of us start growing, and we take a step forward on our personal path. For me, this love has aided me in forgiving the injustices, acts of cruelty, and misunderstanding I witness every day in the animal world. All the misery that animals show me causes me to shudder. There are days I can do nothing but sit down and cry when I see so much unhappiness and injustice. I feel utterly powerless, just one small person who is alone.

I have also been able to forgive myself for my own mistakes that I made before my awareness of love was developed to this extent. I hope that this awareness continues to grow. In all likelihood, it is infinite. Every time I make a communication I learn something and realize that merely an hour earlier I was ignorant, insensitive, and asleep when I thought I was awake.

6

✣

Animals and Their Bodies

The soul is the same in all living things. It is only the body that is different.

HIPPOCRATES

Communication helps us learn how an animal is feeling physically. It allows us to get a grip on their symptoms and their sensations. When we ask them questions and show that we can wait patiently, animals will start providing details with ease. We should remain focused on them and wait. I put myself in their place, and in this way I can feel what they are feeling. We can feel every pain, whether it is acute, stabbing, or has subsided somewhat. We can feel burns, itching sensations, lameness, back pains, and we can determine in what part of the body the problem is located. We can even feel the intense thirst that is sometimes caused by diabetes or by kidneys that are no longer functioning properly or the thirst generated by medications. Sometimes animals show me only what is bothering them the most at that particular time. The most important goal to remember: have patience, learn how to wait, and receive.

❧

I was looking at the photo of Missy, a twelve-year-old, slightly over-weight cat with diabetes. She was black and white with imperturbable blue eyes the color of the large lakes in northern Michigan. She led a quiet life. Her greatest pleasure was purring while sitting on Maria's knees every evening. Yet diabetes had disrupted the humdrum routine of her everyday life. Twice each day Maria gave her the shots she needed, but something was not right.

I therefore closed my eyes and put myself in Missy's place: "I feel like her. I am walking on my velvety paws through the apartment. I can feel my soft, smooth, gleaming fur. I'm at my ease here and feel safe and secure with Maria. But I don't feel very well. All at once I become very hungry, and acid burns my stomach, although it hasn't been long since I had something to eat. This is a very unpleasant sensation. What's more, I feel weak, as if all my blood were turning cold. I feel as though I need to lie down, and it seems as though I can't see very clearly. Perhaps I should eat. I have a 'hole' in my belly. If I sleep, I'll feel better."

There was no reason to stay any longer; I had grasped what the problem was. From Missy's sensations I deduced she was suffering from overly frequent incidents of low blood sugar. After the communication I explained to Maria how Missy was feeling and asked her to go back to her veterinarian so that she could examine the cat's insulin levels. The doctor then adjusted the shots, and Maria called me several days later to tell me that Missy was doing much better. She had more energy and seemed much more balanced.

Another cat, Princess, had failing kidneys and could never quench her thirst. She sat inside the sink so that she could drink from the faucet all day long. I had a photo of her in front of me and entered her skin. I could feel the thirst in my mouth—it was the same feeling caused by human thirst, the same thirst I felt after eating foods that were too salty.

"I can drink until the end of time. The cold water from the faucet flows into my cat mouth, over my tongue, and down my throat, but I'm still thirsty, as if the water does not enter my palette but simply slides off. I have to keep drinking more and more. I have a stomachache, so I stop for a while—but still I feel thirsty. I feel heavy, swollen; my fur feels hot and unpleasant. I want to strip off everything. I stay near the faucet. Hearing the clear drops and feeling the coolness of the wet tile beneath my feet is soothing."

I was Princess while still remaining aware that I was Laila experiencing the body and sensations of Princess. I did not get lost in what I was sensing. When I felt that I had seen enough, I came out of the bloated body of Princess and opened my eyes. I was once more only Laila, but I headed right for the kitchen to drink a tall glass of cold water. All at once the July heat weighed heavy upon me, and the aridity of the desert caused my skin to itch. It is strange how easily we are able to change bodies. Perhaps this is also what happens when we move from one dimension to another. We close our eyes and transform.

I therefore decided to do a healing on poor Princess. Several days later her thirst had diminished substantially, and she was drinking less, but she still preferred to stay close to the faucet, just in case. Her kidneys were still failing, but they did not cause her as much suffering. Princess died several months later.

Kia from Colorado, a bay mare with white stockings, experienced spasms through her entire body whenever anyone mounted her. The veterinarians were perplexed and had no idea where this physiological manifestation might have come from. Poor Kia was utterly miserable. Because of her condition, she often remained penned up, and no one paid any attention to her. She was not taken out for walks or rides. I took her photo and made a communication to see if her trouble was physical or emotional.

Kia was confused. I examined her relationship with her guardian, Cheryl, but could not find anything to point to the horse's unrest.

I then asked Kia to describe her symptoms to me: "Cheryl is on the saddle. We are ready to head out. All at once I feel as if something freezing cold is going through my entire body. It starts in my legs and then climbs into my back through the contraction of my muscles. I try to shake myself to get rid of it. Nothing happens. After, there is a sensation of gripping pincers that causes pain and keeps pinching more and more. My legs are completely contracted, but I try to gallop and shake myself to get rid of this terrible pressure. I feel Cheryl falling to the ground. She yells and I want to stay with her, but I have to get rid of these pincers at any price. I feel her behind me. She's running while shouting my name. I think she's hurt, too . . . Finally it lets up; the pincers are gone. A cold sweat covers my body, my nostrils are smoking, and I'm cold and I feel exhausted . . . Cheryl comes near me. She's limping. She takes me by the bridle. We share the same lack of understanding. What's wrong with me?"

After the communication with Kia, I was also perplexed: What was wrong with her? Could it be a nervous problem? Kia was very apprehensive of being ridden and could not stand anyone being on her back out of fear of experiencing these crises again. This was completely logical. For horses everything is simple. Kia was not being wicked and had no desire to make Cheryl fall.

I explained the entire situation to Cheryl, and we decided to help Kia. I had no idea at this point if we would see any results. I asked the Creator for his aid to heal the mare, and I let him guide me. The spasms disappeared. Yet I asked Cheryl to wait before trying to ride Kia again. It was dangerous, and I did not want her to put herself at risk. It was necessary for Kia to be ready. She had been suffering this way for six years. It is essential to respect an animal in such a situation— but it is admirable to see all the efforts they make and the devotion they display, despite their suffering or fears, in response to our wishes or requirements.

Three weeks later it was possible for Kia to be mounted and ridden. In fact, she seemed quite happy to start going out on excursions again after having felt useless and isolated for these past six years. It is very important for horses to feel as if they are valued. Their lives among us—just as our lives among each other—must have a meaning.

Sonia, a young Chinese woman who had grown up in the United States, called me in an emergency. She was at the veterinarian's because Spike, her two-year-old cat, was extremely ill. It had come on quite suddenly, and no one understood what he had. Even the veterinarian was distressed and mystified. I had worked with Spike before, so I did not need his photo. He was well known for the crazy stunts he pulled. In fact, beneath his innocent little face and large white whiskers, he completely hid what he was actually up to: he was the biggest juvenile delinquent in the neighborhood, and he always dragged other area cats into whatever mischief he was hatching. Yet he was also a little darling. When Sonia turned her back, he would leap silently on to the dining room table—thanks to the fact that his paws were covered by sound-absorbing white socks—and then he would knock to the floor all the cartons containing the leftovers from the Chinese takeout around the corner. Next, all the other cats in the house would leap on the leftovers and share the bounty. Spike's activity always happened so fast that Sonia would not even see him do it!

When Sonia called I could connect with Spike directly to see how he was feeling. His voice was very faint and weak, and he had no clue at all about what had happened to him. The poor cat was not feeling at all playful. I heard his voice—and it was not in the form of a meow. I perceived it in my head, with words, as if it was my own, but I knew it was the cat's thoughts that had transferred from his head to my own. I rapidly described his symptoms to Sonia over the telephone so that she could pass them along to the veterinarian. Most notable was that he had a very strange sensation in his head and that his limbs were gradually being overtaken by a slow paralysis. It was as if poor little Spike was being transformed into a statue of salt, like Lot's wife. All of a sudden the veterinarian shouted out: "He's been poisoned by chocolate!" Sonia then remembered that she had some chocolate cookies in her handbag. The little rascal had climbed up on a chair, knocked her purse to the ground with a deft blow of his paws, and then devoured the cookies! She later found beneath the sofa the remnants of the packaging torn into small pieces. The veterinarian gave him the appropriate treatment immediately, and the pretty little glutton was able to go home, quite happy to be still among the living. He was all set to begin some new adventures.

Miles, a bay horse, had been bitten by a tick and had contracted Lyme disease. He lived with his guardian, Arletta, in a suburb of New York City. A large and handsome horse, Miles had put Arletta through the mill with his fiery and rebellious temperament, but she loved him dearly. When he suffered from Lyme disease, though, the flame in his eyes had died out, he was lethargic, and he was visibly miserable. Arletta had given him time off to do nothing but rest.

I first entered his body to see how he was feeling. I could feel the spasms in all his limbs, particularly in his hind legs and lower back. "I'm tired and so weary, as if my blood had turned into water, and I no longer have the desire to do anything at all. What's more, I feel feverish. I really don't feel well at all. The slightest thing brushing against my skin irritates me. Heat, loud voices—I can't tolerate anything." I came back out of the body of poor Miles.

I prefer to know the exact state of animals before I start working on them, because when I know exactly what they are feeling, my heart opens up, and in this way I become a much clearer channel through which the healing can pass. Often, the healing is made at a distance: with only a photo of the animal and the name and age. When I am inside them, I feel the discomfort in the shape of an animal. At these times I am no longer myself alone. I am Miles, then, while still retaining my awareness of Laila. I do not need to take their illnesses into or upon myself, because these pains remain their property. When I come out of the animal, I surrender everything to the Great Spirit, Creator, and in this way, I come back to myself, limpid and pure.

After several sessions with Miles, his blood tests indicated that he no longer had any signs of the disease. Arletta was thrilled, but I could feel he was still experiencing pain in his limbs. Could these be signs of some kind of relapse? It was only when I saw that he was not having any more physical pain that I stopped working on him. I asked Arletta to allow Miles's rest to continue. Every day she would visit him and bring him treats. Love and attention are what count most in any cure. If the animal retains his desire to live, there is always hope.

A woman from New Jersey named Lynn called me about her husky, Tatonka, who was losing the use of his right eye. Tatonka, a very beautiful dog, had an appearance that was a bit wild and strange: his left eye was brown and his right eye was blue. The specialist did not know how badly Tatonka's vision had deteriorated in the afflicted eye or how intense his pain was. He had been treating him with eye drops to alleviate the tension of his ailing eye. Lynn called me in tears; she had no idea what to do.

I had met Lynn during one of my visits to Philadelphia, so during this communication I could recognize her through Tatonka's eyes. I entered Tatonka and looked at his world: with my good eye, I could see perfectly the house, the wooden staircase, and Lynn. Here are the sensations I perceived through the eyes of this dog, translated into my words.

"Looking out the window of Lynn's room, I can see the trees and all the details of their leaves, but with my other eye, there is a mist, and I can't see anything but shapes. Once, I missed one of the steps on the staircase because I wasn't paying attention. I'm sad and depressed, and Lynn is always worried about me. She talks about an operation for me, but I'm scared. She's even more worried about this than I am. I can sense her fear when she slips into the house. She cries quite often for long periods when she's with her husband, Jim. I try to comfort her, but her sorrow is so great that I don't know what to do. I sit at her feet and look at her. There are days when there's such an acute, stabbing pain in my eye that it feels as though there are knives inside it. I try to pull them out with my paw, but it doesn't work. So then I hide under her bed."

Tatonka could also show me the exact effect the drops had on his sight: "Yes, the drops help a little. Afterward I can see a bit better." Lynn was a psychotherapist. She thought that there might be something that she was refusing to look at in her own life and that this had caused Tatonka to develop glaucoma in one of his eyes. This was possible—she was almost certainly right that everything depends on how we choose to look at the world—but in the meantime, Tatonka was suffering. So Lynn decided to have an operation performed on Tatonka's eye. It was successful.

In order to know the feelings of an animal, we should leave our own ego behind and slide into him. Our mind, our spirit, is intangible and can go wherever it likes. Of course, out of respect, we should always ask an animal's permission beforehand; we cannot do this without asking. What will sustain us is the intense desire to provide an animal with help. This will lift our spirits and allow us to project ourselves inside an animal so that we can feel what he is feeling. This desire to give help is absolutely essential: it is the drawing of the bow that allows the arrow to hit its target.

I once made a communication with a thirteen-year-old white Labrador. Beau had bone cancer in one of his front paws. His guardian, a French woman named Michelle who lived in Los Angeles, adored him. She wanted to know if he would rather get "the shot" (be put to sleep) or have the diseased limb amputated. In cases like this I do not enter the animal's body in my usual fashion. I still feel their feelings as my own, but I remain on the outside. It causes me too much pain to experience their suffering directly. Michelle and her husband brought the Labrador to my studio. My dogs did not even bark when he came into the garden. It was as if his presence was emanating something very beautiful and powerful.

Beau was magnificent and handsome. When I touched his soft white fur, I could feel my heart melting. I sat on the ground, and he rested his head on my knees as if we had known each other forever. His brown eyes brimmed with love. He had so much of it to give, despite how miserable he felt! I was tranquil with him and totally at peace. Beau's death was imminent, but he wanted to go on living a bit longer to help Michelle, who was suffering from multiple sclerosis. His handsome face tried to conceal his illness and his fear. Beau did not want to get the shot. Perhaps all the time he had remaining was a month, a year—I could not be certain. "Please, tell them that I need to stick around a little longer . . . It's too soon for me to leave. Michelle still needs me, she still needs the love I give her, she isn't ready."

Yet the cancer spread rapidly and caused Beau terrible suffering. The decision was therefore made to amputate the limb. After the operation I made a communication with Beau. He felt happy and free. He could still feel the phantom leg, which sometimes caused him to stumble, but he had no more pain. He learned to adapt to his new life. One day Michelle brought him to visit me, pulling him along in a children's little red wagon. She never let him out of her sight; she brought him with her everywhere she went. He seemed to be smiling—he was very pleased with himself for having outwitted the specter of death. When he left, Beau looked into my eyes as if to say: "I know. Don't say anything. Just pretend, for me as much as for her . . ." I never saw him again. He died six months later.

A woman called me from Switzerland about her black cat, Negrito, who was experiencing epileptic fits. He was still very young. I entered into him, but because the sensation of the fit was so unpleasant, I came back out immediately. Animals are able to show me the sensation of a crisis, even if they went through it several months earlier. I have wondered if this might be evidence of a memory on the cellular level, because the crisis isn't actually taking place at the time that I am making the communication. Nevertheless, it feels as if it was in the present. With communication I am able to project myself into the past or the future;

time no longer exists. When I do a healing on an animal, I project him into a happy and healthy body, free of any disease. I enter the animal and become a healthy body that can gallop, run, frolic, or fly. At this moment in the animal's imagination, the illness is erased as if it never existed; it becomes a vague and blurry memory, like a nightmare that is quickly forgotten upon awakening.

I think we are able to dismantle the memory in this way if the animal is in agreement to let go of the disease. Negrito panicked at the thought of having another fit. He had experienced several already at regular intervals, and he knew that another one could begin without warning. I felt a pang of anguish at the sight of the fear in this black-as-night, soft, and silky body. Negrito had decided that the best course would be to move as little as possible in case the enemy returned. He waited, his nerves on edge, like someone expecting an invisible and dangerous foe. We see shadows moving through the night, although nothing is there, and in our fear, we hear footsteps in the corridor. Negrito did not play anymore—he did not run about, and he refused to eat. He simply waited, prepared to attack in defense of himself—but his enemy was on the inside.

Fortunately, it proved possible to cure Negrito. Perhaps we owed thanks to fate or to divine intervention. It did not require many healing sessions. It is truly a pleasure to know that you have been heard by the Creator, Great Spirit, and to see the physical results down here, on our earth. Negrito no longer waited expectantly. The enemy was not coming back, because the Creator had slammed the door in his face. The little cat now allowed himself the pleasure of frolicking through the entire house and doing whatever is natural for a cat his age: he leaped, raced around, climbed things, knocked over objects, stole food, left little cat footprints all over Madame's papers, and was constantly brushing up along her legs and emitting loud meows that prevented her from paying attention to anything else. All at once it was as if this illness had never existed and that the memory of it had become faint like a nightmare quickly forgotten.

❧

A woman named Clara called me on behalf of her wolf hybrid, Beauty, who was sick. She thought that Beauty might have been poisoned. The veterinarian was not at all sure about the symptoms. He thought she might be suffering from ulcers, but her condition had deteriorated suddenly. Beauty moaned and refused to eat. It was obvious that she was suffering, so Clara brought her to see me.

Beauty's bloodline had very little crossbreeding with dogs and her coat was thick and a gleaming light brown color. She was a beautiful animal, with her narrow, gold eyes. Clara had warned me that Beauty was not very sociable, and because she was sick, she certainly would not be on her best behavior. I should especially take pains to ensure that none of my curious cats stuck even the tips of their noses into my studio. From the moment we met, Beauty and I formed a very strong connection. Perhaps she had recognized my affinity with wolves. Communicating with a wolf was very different. She was extremely intelligent, and her senses were much more acute than those of dogs. Telepathically she was extremely advanced and reacted to my slightest thought.

Beauty was in front of me, lying calmly on the floor of my studio. She understood perfectly that I was there to help her. I placed one hand on her luxurious pelt, closed my eyes, and slipped inside her. At first I felt spasms in her belly as well as a burning sensation. I next received an image of a hot dog that someone had given her. I could taste it in my mouth. There was a whitish acidic powder inside it that had a funny taste. "Too late. I had already swallowed it. This mix burns me terribly, and I am hurting terribly, as if there is a fire burning inside my stomach."

I came out of the wolf's body and started searching mentally for the origin of this white powder. It was a chemical—a household cleaning product—and I could see that it came in something that looked like a plastic bottle with a yellow label and black writing. It also appeared that someone had deliberately fed this product to the wolf on several occasions. Clara immediately recognized the product as one that she had in her home. From this she deduced that it was clearly a case of poisoning, and she identified the guilty party: a woman who had recently been living with her and was very jealous of Clara. They often quarreled. She did not give me any more details. Perhaps it was a story concerning a man or female rivalry—or maybe this woman thought she was Lucrezia Borgia. She had taken her revenge on the animal whom Clara loved best—her magnificent wolf, Beauty. Happily, Beauty was healed.

With horses, by feeling the balance of the legs, we can often detect a problem with the way the horseshoes are positioned on their feet. I am extremely sensitive to the sensation and equilibrium of the legs of a horse, perhaps because I am a dancer. Mentally I place the horse in front of me during a communication, and I make him walk. In this way I can easily feel if there is a problem in his legs or haunches. For example, in a Spanish mare named Belleza, I had the clear sensation that there was a cavity in her back left hoof—like the broken heel of a shoe. This created the sensation that one leg was longer than the other—a sensation that was very annoying when she walked. The horse's guardian actually told me that her mare had a problem with this hoof. The blacksmith then placed on her hooves horseshoes made especially for her so that she could recover her balance. Belleza was very anxious to return to her physical well-being.

In another case I was able to detect a problem that was navicular in origin: the horse that was limping showed me sharp stabbing pains located in the center of his right foot when he put it on the ground. The veterinarian confirmed my diagnosis. Through communication it is possible to transmit to individuals the physical sensations their animals are experiencing. I must note again that I do not have any special power. Everyone can do what I do, and it can be learned. By practicing, anyone will be able to help animals and thereby prevent future complications.

This often makes it possible for us to get them to the veterinarian in time. The veterinarian can detect a disease by performing tests and taking blood, but he does not know in advance how his patients are feeling. For example, through communication it is possible to prevent horses from getting colic. I had warned the guardian of Leonard, a polite Hungarian bay who lived in Los Angeles, that her horse was at risk of developing colic. He was too stressed and tired, and he had already begun to experience cramps. I asked her to give him time off to rest, but she absolutely wanted him to take part in the next scheduled competition. Five days later, he was in the clinic because of colic. This was a visit that could have been entirely avoided.

Often a guardian is aware that an animal is suffering from an illness, but he does not know what the illness is. The animal has a different expression on his face, he is not lively, he sleeps all day, he looks tired. What is going on?

Sometimes animals mask their symptoms out of the necessity to survive or to spare any pain for the person with whom they live. In cases like these, the cause is much harder to find. Because animals cannot express themselves, it is necessary to feel what they are feeling.

I knew a white, nineteen-year-old dog, Scooter, who was the superman of the canine species. From time to time his guardian brought him to me for treatments. He had survived being hit by a car, numerous rescue shelters, cancer, a chronic heart ailment, a kidney infection, an ulcer in his left eye, a fall from my massage table, and countless other accidents. His most recent misadventure took place near Washington, where he fell from a cliff. The firemen were called, and they found him unscathed, strolling nonchalantly through the bushes at the foot of the cliff.

He had the personality of an old curmudgeon, as if he felt he had been ill-served by life. When I talked to him, he showed me only several troubles: just a few pains on the left leg where he had surgery. After each treatment he would rejuvenate and appear as if he were five years younger. His capacity for regeneration was so strong.

If no one kept a close watch on him, he would often disappear, going off on his own to see just what the world had to offer him on that day. He always had an experience on these travels, but he would emerge innocent and unscathed, like a newborn puppy. He would always arise, wide-eyed and a little astonished, as if life's tribulations had no power to touch him. He did not even appear to realize what had happened to him, as if every strange occurrence was just a regular part of life. Scooter was a true model for learning how to meet life's challenges. Thanks to him, I discovered a great deal every time I saw him.

Some animals disguise their symptoms to protect the person they love. Popi was a pretty brown dog, about ten years old, who had big, black-velvet eyes. She had been stricken by cancer and had several tumors in her stomach and lungs. Randi loved her more than anything else in the world. She would bring her by my studio regularly for treatments. Popi absolutely had to live. "I could not go on living without her!" she told me. Yet the veterinarian, a highly regarded specialist in Los Angeles, told Randi that her dog did not have much longer to live. Despite this grim diagnosis, Popi went on to live another three years. What was most surprising is that she did not seem to note her condition. She leaped up onto the massage table, her eyes bright, totally content to be getting all dolled up. She barked at anyone who came near the studio, chased after squirrels as if she was still a puppy, and liked to play with a ball.

When I asked her to describe her symptoms, she showed me nothing. I tried to put myself in her place, and still I saw nothing. Seized by doubt, I wondered if I had lost all my abilities—but she simply did not want me to know about her illness. This was simply out of the question. She wanted to remain on this earth for as long as possible for Randi's sake—because her guardian loved her passionately. I, too, became very attached to her. I knew that she could not be cured but that it was possible to give her more time and to relieve the symptoms. In fact, these healing sessions with Popi were for the purpose of allowing Randi to say her good-bye little by little.

Once I began a treatment, Randi would fall asleep at the same time as Popi. This affirmed that the work was being done on Randi.

Eventually, though, it was time for Popi to go. I could sense it. The last time that she came to my studio, she stood up after the session and—this was unusual—gave me a very long look with her deep eyes. Normally she shook all over, eager to leave and chase the squirrels in my garden. Randi told me, "Look, she is telling you good-bye!" I knew that Popi's gaze was a good-bye forever: "I have to leave now, and thank you, thank you for Randi!"

I was heading to France the next day. Popi died while I was gone, although she appeared to be in good health. I could not keep her here.

We do become another being when communicating, but it is possible to look inside another body while retaining our awareness and our ability to observe. How? As I've said, we should always have an animal's permission, and we must always project ourselves toward the Creator. It is important to enter into communication with great integrity and the intention of helping an animal. In order to learn this work, it is essential to receive training from an experienced person. Animals are aware that they do not feel well, but they do not know the specific disease or malady that is troubling them. Because of this awareness of feeling on the part of the animal, it is possible to look inside a bone, the bloodstream, or an organ.

I communicated with Aube, a mare who was pregnant. She was exhausted and out of shape, and I could see a problem for her fetus. Aube, who was aware of difficulties, did not know if her pregnancy would come to term. Her unease caused even greater stress upon her immune system. Looking inside her blood, I saw something odd in the corpuscles: they looked like little patches, but endowed with a consciousness. There were several of these patches in every corpuscle. I then suggested to Aube's guardian that she have the horse's blood analyzed. It turned out that the mare had piroplasmosis* Because she was pregnant, it was out of the question that she be given the specified medical treatment for this dis-

---

*[A tick-borne protozoal infection of horses and related equines. —*Ed.*]

ease. I asked the Great Spirit, Creator of All, to help her. She gave birth to a perfectly healthy colt.

I have looked in the intestines of horses on several occasions to detect if they have worms, bacteria, or parasites. I do not always know how to differentiate them, but each has a consciousness. Sometimes I can see the worms. They do not present a very appetizing picture, but there they are, swarming inside the intestine, happy to be alive! When I try to speak to them, they are very stubborn and have no intention of moving to a new location. They find themselves very much at ease in such a grand hotel—no complaints from that party! Threats and pleas alike are futile. I have yet to find a means of getting them to leave.

A veterinarian once asked me to take a look at her dog. She did not share her diagnosis with me so that she could verify if it matched with my communication. In examining the dog's blood, I saw that the white corpuscles appeared to be gathered together densely, and they stuck tightly to each other, somewhat like a ball. The red corpuscles appeared weak. I know nothing about medicine, so I simply described to the veterinarian what I saw. She confirmed that she had thought the dog suffered from a kind of leukemia, and that what I described was definitely the appearance the blood takes in this disease.

For bones, observation is just as important. If there is a fracture, for instance, it is possible to see what type and how serious it is. By looking at the fractured leg of a Spanish horse, I could see that it was only cracked and would heal on its own. It is also possible to feel the extent to which a diseased organ can heal itself or if it needs assistance.

I do not have a very good grasp of anatomy, though I am always trying to expand my knowledge of the subject. Yet looking inside a body is also a form of communication. A whole mind, an entire consciousness, can find a way to "speak" in this way. We communicators can feel the whole because we become part of the animal's whole.

7

Unique or Strange Cases

*You know, in the beginning, men and animals lived very
close together, eating and sleeping together. This was in the
beginning and it was like heaven on earth for a long time.
The human being could speak to the four-legged people, the
two-legged people, and the people with two wings.*

DHYANI YWAHOO, CHEROKEE

An animal communicator is like the Sherlock Holmes of the animal
world—there are always mysteries to be solved, and mysteries are exciting; they can be a real challenge. I like the cases that nobody has been
able to solve, because they force me to push past my limits and go much
deeper. In my practice I sometimes pose questions to the Great Spirit,
Creator, in search of answers that go beyond the animal. I believe that
every being living on earth is connected to the whole. With the Great
Spirit's consent, we are able to gain access to all the answers that may
help restore a lost balance.

The trick is finding the key that enables us to gain access to this
space of answers. The key can be different for each individual, and it
can be obtained through meditation, faith, the practice of a certain
technique, revelation, or a loving state. In all cases it works first and

foremost through silence, listening, and the certitude that we are being heard. Communication with an animal naturally opens the door to another dimension, because we have already opened our heart.

This is how I proceed with my communications, always knowing that there are thousands of different possible results. I always come to results in this way: First, I breathe and center myself around my heart in a state of marvelous tranquillity. It sometimes takes time to reach this sensation of peace—the amount of time depends on how my day has been and the level of stress I have experienced. Through continuity and habit, we can learn to reach this state quickly. I practice every morning and in the afternoon or evening, so if I have questions about an animal that require answers, I am almost always ready to find them.

When I feel as if I am permeated with peace, I ask to communicate. I always wait for this sensation of peace and truth, then I ask for information to come to me by way of the Creator. It is as if a flood of light invades me, both entering and surrounding me. Customarily, it is as if a white substance fills my heart and belly. It is extremely comforting. On some days this light is quite vast and on others, it is extremely small. Size depends upon my mood and situation, but it serves as a signal: if I can feel this peace, no matter how minimal its presence, I can then formulate my question, because I know that I am being heard (though, of course, we are always being heard). After asking, I stay in this place without saying anything, and I wait for an answer.

Sometimes the response is quite clear, and other times I can barely understand it. I then have to say: "I am not sure of the answer! I cannot hear it!" Sometimes I ask the same question three times, just to be certain. I spent a long time learning how to discern what I was hearing. To be even more cautious, I ask the same question again on another day, so that I can be certain of the information in the answer. Finally, my heart must be in agreement with the answer I hear—and the answer should be accompanied by a sensation of love. For instance, if what I hear is, "Go throw yourself off the top of a cliff," something is not right! The answer will come only with a great deal of love. In addition, there is always a sensation of help and compassion in the answer. We are never told: "You have to do this or that . . ." Instead, we are imperceptibly guided toward a purpose: to give help. It is always up to us to make the decision of what should be done next.

I practice. Every day, I ask. There are moments when I do not hear anything, so I wait. It is always an experiment—but we have to make the effort. Through the process I learn greater discernment. Through validation, I gather faith. What is important: knowing that we are listened to and that someone will answer us. In our Judeo-Christian tradition we are accustomed to praying and asking while being convinced that no one hears us and that our prayers will never be granted. Yet we continue to pray nonetheless—in case the Creator deigns to listen to us. We may think that we are not worthy to be heard, but we continue praying, because we have been taught to do so.

All it takes, however, is a single key—tiny though it may be—to enter into a marvelous and magical universe formed by the very substance of the Creator, which is love. He is this universe, and we form part of him. We are able to speak with him. We are able to breathe him in and integrate him at any time, because the sacred is within us. Enough of the mute "good Lord" with his white beard and his throne, the Lord who wears earplugs made of clouds!

I was called about a Hungarian horse, Trooper, who lived in the outskirts of New York. He often caused his rider, Heidi, to fall off, yet this extremely sweet and gentle horse respected her. The situation was incomprehensible. Already, three of Heidi's ribs had been fractured in the riding ring. Trooper had also made his trainer fall, but the trainer was more agile and managed to save himself from injury. When a ride began, Trooper was always calm, but he would soon become completely nervous. By communicating with him, I was able to see quite clearly the state he was in, but I was unable to unearth its origin. It had nothing to do with Heidi, the trainer, the place, or his past. I asked questions and probed deeper—but nothing!

I then heard the word *herbs*. I thought this came not from Trooper, but from somewhere else. I asked Heidi, then, if she gave him herbs. It turned out that she did: an entire blend of herbs—a mix that can be bought in health food stores—to provide energy. Apparently the blend was too strong for him and caused too much stimulation—thus, his nervousness. She therefore stopped giving him the herbs, and three weeks later Trooper was much calmer and his muscles were relaxed. Now there is no problem at all with riding him.

With another guardian instead of Heidi—someone with less patience—he might have been sold.

I have noticed that many people use herbs because they are somewhat in style. Under normal circumstances you should give an animal—over a short period of time—a blend containing only three herbs at most. In nature a sick animal will instinctively stop eating his or her regular diet and select herbs that have healing properties. In no case would an animal ever take a blend of thirty-six herbs in a capsule! He would choose herbs found in his natural environment, instead of those from the other side of the planet.

During a workshop in Haute-Savoie, Magali talked to us about her cat, Mouche, who every autumn would develop a huge knot of fur on her back. Mouche was very cute—a black cat with a white chest—but she was also very shy and fearful. Upon the arrival of the people taking the course, she would disappear and hide somewhere in the house. Every September, once the tenth of the month had passed, she would develop this problem. It was a complete mystery. People thought it might be related to climate, allergies, painting, even the presence of evil spirits in the house . . . who would put in an appearance only in September!

When I communicate with an animal, I sometimes hear words that do not necessarily come out of his mouth. For their part, animals—no more than we—do not know why they are sick. They are not veterinarians who wear fur coats—yet when we learn to listen to them, we often receive information that comes to help them. Perhaps these words are from spirits or guides who speak in these instances. I know for certain only that if we remain—with the animal present in front of us—in an attitude of neutral and silent waiting with the intention of helping, we can sometimes receive a few of these words. Often, these few are just enough to unravel the plot.

So I closed my eyes for Mouche and clearly stated my intention of obtaining an answer. I heard: "School, return to school." What in the world could that mean? I did not understand it at all—cats do not go to school! I then heard, "Ask Magali about the school." Magali paused. Silence. She just looked at me with her blue eyes. All my students were watching. The silence grew heavier. Maybe I had gone completely crazy. . . . But all of a sudden, her face changed color, and then she remembered: In September one year, when Magali had to go back to school, her mother almost died. She had to be admitted to a hospital, and no one knew if she could be cured. The mother thus found another woman to take care of the house for Magali's father, and she organized the placing of her children in the homes of different people. Magali found herself all alone in someone else's home, without her brothers and sisters, during her mother's convalescence. She felt abandoned, fearful, stressed.

Magali soon began to think that every September complications would occur in her life—and everything went wrong. It was always an extremely difficult period. This stress was inside her, on her—everywhere. Mouche absorbed it for her, and it reappeared in the form of this ball on the cat's back. Magali realized that it was all connected, and she concluded: "The ball will not be coming back now!" All at once Mouche popped out of her hiding place and walked into the center of the circle formed by my students. She even begged for caresses, and I received the benefit of petting her beautiful silky fur and getting a handsome purr in return. When September came around again, the ball of fur did not.

Chris called me one day about his dog, Peanut, who was scared of the daylight. No one knew why. He had had Peanut, black as night, since the dog was little. During daylight hours, Peanut would hide inside the house. It was impossible to convince him to put a paw outside—not even if a squirrel appeared in the yard! Chris could take him for walks only late at night. The veterinarian had been unable to find anything wrong. Even Peanut's vision seemed normal. It was a mystery. Chris had convinced himself that Peanut's terror was due to seeing spirits or ghosts . . . Yet, though this would be an appealing explanation for Edgar Allan Poe, it runs counter to what all the stories tell us: ghosts come out only at night.

Peanut did not know how to explain to me why he had this fear, but I could feel his terror when it began to grow light. So I put myself in his place in order to see for myself. This is what I felt inside Peanut: "The light of day makes my eyes hurt very much. All my visual sensations are amplified a thousand times in daylight. It's both dazzling and very strange, like thousands of luminous needles. I see too much, I hear too much. The garden transforms itself into a terrifying jungle. There are huge shadows, beings that threaten me, strange noises. It's like being in some sort of apocalyptic movie. At night my vision returns to normal. Night's thick shadow protects me and envelops me. Everything calms down then; I feel peaceful and tranquil. Each of the smells is in its proper place. I can follow them and am happy."

We could never uncover the reason why he felt this way. It may have been a result of inbreeding. But Peanut still harbors fears of daylight, and Chris still has to take him on nocturnal walks.

Jordana called me on behalf of her horse, Bliss, who lived with her in Santa Barbara, California. He was a magnificent, completely white horse. He had a habit of weaving (a kind of swaying from one end to the other, a sign of high anxiety) whenever he was separated from another horse. It did not matter which horse; it did not necessarily have to be a frequent companion. I looked at the black-and-white photo of him that I had been given. Bliss was galloping in the ring with Jordana on his back—very elegant. I closed my eyes, met him, and began a communication.

His anxiety had nothing at all to do with Jordana or another horse. He seemed fine and was well and affectionately cared for. What, then, was the reason for this puzzling behavior? I probed deeper, I asked my questions again and again, and I waited. This made no sense: I could feel his anxiety plainly as the sensation of a lump in his throat, a sense of panic in his belly, and a cold sweat over his entire body.

I remained with him in his anxiety and accompanied him, pushing deeper into the heart of the emotion. His anxiety climbed higher and higher. He was ready to explode and break everything. All at once he was in the middle of an earthquake. He was five years old. Here are the sensations that I perceived through him: "It's night. I become terrified. The ground is rumbling beneath my feet. There are ferocious beasts that are going to try to kill me as well as the other horses in the stable. Everything is shaking. The noise is terrifying; the horses are neighing in panic and rearing as they try to get out. There is no way out. A panicked terror grips my belly, and I find myself all alone, cornered. Where are the others?"

It seems that several horses did manage to get out. When I spoke about this with Jordana, she told me that actually, when Bliss was five years old, he was not in Santa Barbara but in a suburb of San Francisco when a terrible earthquake occurred. She knew nothing else about her horse's past. Following my communication with Bliss, I deduced that this was the source of his anxiety. Every time another horse went away from his stable, it triggered the memory he had of his separation from his companion horses during the earthquake—his fear, his isolation, and his vulnerability. Armed with this knowledge, I was able to do emotional work with him. With images and sensations we went through each of his traumatic episodes until he was able to let go of them. I accompanied him to the bottom of each emotion until he managed to free himself from its charge.

After this work Jordana called me to say that everything was going well. Bliss was experiencing only very short and rare episodes of weaving.

8

The Messenger Birds

*The birds of your planet are often messengers or translators
of Non-Physical energy . . . [this is] because the birds are
mobile, they are everywhere, and they are willing . . .*

JERRY AND ESTHER HICKS,
THE TEACHINGS OF ABRAHAM

Animals communicate—we have only to listen to them. One day I
was teaching a course in the Jura region. We were in a sort of cafeteria. Outside it was cold and raining buckets. A little bird, a wagtail,
came to the window and watched us. Everyone noticed it. He seemed
to be holding court over the premises with plenty of self-assurance. He
perched on the edge of the window, looked curiously over our little
group with his piercing eyes, and then arranged his feathers with his
tiny beak before suddenly flying off. Twenty minutes later, he returned,
circled the cafeteria several times and perched once more on the windowsill. He seemed to be saying to us: "Ah, you are still there!" It was
as if we were children staging a play. The group was in full rehearsal and
quite busy. The bird pirouetted into the air and came back from time
to time just to cast a glance through the window to assure himself that
all was well.

The second day of the course, after lunch, the bird began tapping on the window with great insistence—short, regular taps. We looked at him uncomprehendingly, but he did not leave; he continued tapping as if to say: "Come on, open up, come on, it's me!" So we opened the window, despite the cold, thinking that the bird might be hungry. One of the students put some breadcrumbs on the windowsill, but he immediately flew away. It was not bread that he wanted.

At this moment, one of the students realized what was going on. She recalled that it was necessary to open the window regularly because the cafeteria's coal heating system was not functioning properly. Our little wagtail had saved us all from a fine case of carbon monoxide poisoning! The bird reappeared at the window later in the day, as if he was making sure that everything was all right. We were all enormously grateful to him. He was our little feathered guardian angel.

A woman called me about a small bird named Sunshine. He had very pretty white and silver feathers. His guardian was extremely ill, suffering from cancer that did not allow her to leave her bed. My communication with Sunshine was intended to help find out if the bird would like to be adopted by Patty, a friend of this woman, or if he wanted to stay with his current guardian. I took his photo into my hands, closed my eyes, and slipped into their house.

It smelled of mildew and death. Everything was dark, heavy. There was a large, tiger-striped tomcat wandering around the apartment, not knowing what to do with himself. I approached Sunshine's cage and saw his feathers gleaming in the darkness. I could sense the bed close by and the presence of the ill woman. I received a thought in the form of a fine, thin voice telling me: "I want to stay with her until the end."

Sunshine had a very beautiful voice, and he loved to sing. When he sang the entire house seemed to fill with joy and light. Even the cat listened to him. There were no longer any bars, there was no more sorrow—everything turned in to infinite space. Perhaps he sang to cure his guardian, but it was not working. At this time Sunshine was not singing. As his guardian's illness progressed, the house became darker and increasingly silent. Sometimes Sunshine communicated with the tomcat, who groomed himself beneath the cage every morning. They did not have much to say. "We know that she's going to leave us soon. It's Patty who gives us food and something to drink every day."

The ambulance came to take the woman to the hospital. The next day Patty came to the house to feed Sunshine and the tomcat, but when she approached the cage, Sunshine was lying there, his beautiful feathers all stiff and his beautiful voice extinguished forever. He had flown off to accompany his guardian toward the light. I cried when Patty told me this story, because I, too, had been touched by Sunshine's voice. And then I thought of the old Chinese proverb: "A bird does not sing because it has an answer; it sings because it has a song." I believe that birds know interspecies communication. I think all animals know it, but it seems that for birds this understanding is entirely natural—perhaps because they have the possibility of moving so easily between heaven and earth, perhaps because their spirits are so light.

I made a communication with a dapple-gray horse named Star who was quite old and was suffering from health problems. He lived one hour outside of Los Angeles. Star showed me that for a companion he had a pretty little bird who visited him every day. The horse lived all by himself in a large meadow—not at all natural for a horse. He found this solitude quite difficult; he would have preferred to have other horses around him. The companion bird was the sole presence in his life. I felt that Star's biggest concern was that he not abandon this bird friend in the event that he died. This surprised me. When I spoke with Star's guardian, Carolyn, she told me that a bird actually flew down every day to perch on the horse's right shoulder, and he would stay there for hours. In addition, this bird was blue!

I was staying with some friends in southern France. It was a beautiful evening tempered by the heat of noon. A horse dentist, Ludovic, accompanied me, and we were looking at two horses in a field, when all of a sudden I felt a tugging at my back, as if someone was pulling on my shirt. I turned around. Behind the wall of the grounds, a little jay looked at me. I went toward him. He was hopping up and down with great difficulty on a pile of wood and trying to climb up the wall of the house. Once I drew quite close to him, he looked at me intently with his little eyes, and I could hear clearly: "Help me, help me!" Initially, I thought the bird might be injured, because he was shivering with fear. I could feel that he was thirsty and at the edge of complete exhaustion. I next perceived these sensations: "I've lost my mama. Where is my mama? Help me!" It wrung my heart, but I was not sure what I could do.

I later learned that one of the women visiting our hosts on this day had seen the little bird after breakfast and had told him: "Go see Laila. She will help you!" So the little jay had hopped his way all around the large house to look for me in the field, where I was with the horses. This must have taken him a great deal of time, because night was already falling. Wearily, he left to conceal himself in the bushes behind the house. Despite the tugging at my heart, I said: "Perhaps it would be better to let nature take its course. I will not meddle in this." But the dentist next to me said: "Ask what you should do." So I directed a request to the Creator, Great Spirit.

I could hear very clearly inside me, "Help it!" and I knew intuitively what to do. Ludovic trapped the bird with his hands, then he rolled a cloth around him and gave him to me. He had grabbed the bird gently without hurting it. Once the little jay found himself in Ludovic's hands, he calmed down immediately. I was surprised. I had seen my dentist friend work his magic many times with horses, but I had no idea that it worked just as well on nestlings!

I communicated with the tiny jay to learn what had happened to him. He showed me in pictures how he had fallen from the nest he shared with three brothers and sisters. He had suddenly found himself in full sunlight on a burning, hard ground. There were tiny pebbles beneath his feet. He was extremely anxious and filled with distress: "Where is my mama?" He did not know how to fly.

When I described the situation to my friends, they were immediately certain on what side of the house the nest was located. Painters had been working there and must have moved the nest accidentally. It was the very spot where he had been seen by the houseguest that morning: the facade facing south, which received full sunlight. I then tried to communicate with the mother from a distance. She was busy taking care of the three other nestlings and rebuilding a nest for them. She knew that the lost nestling was safe and sound. I felt responsible for this little jay, but I had no idea what I could do to help him. I knew I had to take steps quickly, though, because night was falling. Once again, the dentist whispered to me: "Ask! You will be told!" I knew that we had to hydrate the bird—give him water to drink with something small like an eyedropper. I also knew we had to keep him warm inside during the night. It was out of the question to leave him outside; he would never last the night. Don't worry, I told myself, everything would work out fine. The nestling would find his mother the next day.

Ludovic went in search of a small syringe intended for horses, and with infinite patience, focusing on getting the bird to open his beak, he gave him one drop of water after another. The bird's eyes were half closed, and we felt that hydration was having a regenerative effect on him: tiny sounds emerged from his throat after each drop. Very rapidly he regained his strength. Once reinvigorated, he chose Ludovic as his adoptive father. He amused himself by climbing up and down the dentist's shoulders, then climbing over the nape of his neck and giving his cheeks affectionate little pecks. He must have been thinking that he was a bit different, this featherless father! Meanwhile, it had grown late, and it was now time for bed. We used my sweater to make a small nest for the bird, but he refused to nod off, so I took him into my hands and said a prayer—and he immediately plunged into a deep sleep. He spent the entire night with me in my room.

The next day, when I opened my eyes, I saw him staring motionlessly at the face of a wooden statue of the Chinese goddess of compassion, Quan Yin. I had noticed this beautiful statue the night before as I was getting ready for bed. The tiny jay didn't even let out a tiny peep. I went in search of Ludovic. He came back in with me, picked up the bird in the palm of his hand, and opened the large glass window that looked over the garden. The little jay, which had not known how to fly the day before, soared away into the glow of the rising sun. I felt he would head right back to the mother jay.

Had the goddess of compassion taught him how to fly during the night? I realized that I, too, had been given a message: "Listen to your heart. Let yourself be guided, and the Creator will give you wings to use in going toward the light." Every life is precious and every breath is unique. Every being has his own place and purpose in the sacred circle of life. The opportunity may arise in our life when we are given a valuable gift: to save a life or help an animal find its way back to the Creator.

One day I was giving a dance performance at the World Culture Festival at the Getty Museum. The stage was set up on a large patio. It was the beginning of the evening during June, and there were around two hundred spectators. I had been having a feeling of inner emptiness for a while. I had received so much, and now I was going through a dark night of the soul, the night described so perfectly by St. John of the Cross. I could no longer understand anything, and I doubted everything. Before I began my dance, I looked up at the sky and said: "Creator, I am dancing now for you. Please give me a sign. Tell me it's not over and that there's a light at the end of this tunnel. Tell me that I'm being heard and that I've not been abandoned."

I was fully in the middle of the choreographed piece, dancing the *letra de la solea,* when all at once I saw that Jesus Montoya, a Gypsy, had stopped singing. He was looking at the sky and saying: *Mira, una paloma blanca!* (Look, a white dove!) All the musicians and dancers looked up, and the *palmas* (hands, clapping of hands) came to a halt. We were all frozen in place on the stage, like statues of salt. A brief moment of silence was suspended in time, and my arms were still lifted toward the sky in a *brazeo* (dance of the arms). I looked up to the left, and there in the sky was a beautiful white dove.

With his wings fully extended, he sketched two lazy circles high above our heads, then he suddenly vanished. Jesus Montoya made the sign of the cross and began singing again. I started dancing again, my heart bursting with joy, my feet in their dance shoes soaring over the stage, and the rhythms responding like the songs of birds. Applause broke out.

The dove had come down that evening for me and for all of those present, and it had a message for each one there.

9

❧

The Primordial Language

He who looks outward is dreaming. He who looks inward is waking up.

CARL JUNG

Animal communication takes place through telepathy. We all can communicate in this form. It is our first language, and it preexists speech. We are capable of feeling perceptions and information about animals because we all form part of this same field, which physicists call the *quantum field*. It is through our education and our society that this language has been buried deep within us, and it is as if we had known this language when we were very young children and forgot it as we grew. To rediscover this form of communication it is important to go within ourselves in silence and relearn how to listen. Once the "machine" has been turned on again, telepathy becomes easy.

During my life with the Gypsies of Spain, I observed that they possess a more acute intuition than what is considered normal. Because I was a flamenco dancer I spent time with them and lived with them—and I had the unprecedented luck to be accepted by the Gypsies and their people. It was they who passed on to me the art of flamenco. It is very rare for a Gypsy to accept a *gadjo* (a non-Gypsy) inside his family, and I will be eternally grateful to them for this. This is how at the same time that I learned dance I also learned another way of being. The Gypsies *capture* what lies behind words, because there is a large space in which travel impressions, images, and meanings that often have nothing to do with words. Sometimes the Gypsies said things that were different from what they thought—not underlying things, but something else entirely. When they listened to someone talking, they did so inside the space that is behind words.

There are many subjects that are taboo to Gypsies, and we must sense what they are before we commit an error. It is very easy to offend someone without even realizing that you have offended! There is a way of communicating that they recognize implicitly as the norm—but is not at all the norm for someone coming from another culture. By living with the Gypsies, therefore, I was able to sharpen my intuitive capabilities. I learned to decode the meaning of hidden thoughts and all the sensations that a situation radiated. I do not know if this form of telepathy was kept by this people out of the need to survive in a hostile world or if they simply preserved this intuitive faculty from one generation to the next.

I lived with La Chana in Premia de Mar, a village near Barcelona. She taught me dance steps in her kitchen while she prepared aioli* for the next meal. Behind the steps there was also an entire body of knowledge, the tradition of her people, which I absorbed without even realizing it. La Chana caught everything behind words and behavior. She told me, "I can also understand animals"—and it was true. The Gypsies have a tradition of cooperation with animals, especially horses. Perhaps this ability stemmed from a difficult childhood in which she was kidnapped by a Gypsy at a young age and forced to marry soon afterward. Her perceptions had been awakened by her survival instinct. She then became a great *maestra* of flamenco.

She had never gone to school. At that time in Spain, Gypsies were not permitted to attend school. Those, such as La Chana, who knew

---

*[Aioli is a Provencal garlic mayonnaise sauce. —*Ed.*]

how to read, had learned it on their own or from another member of their family—much as they learned flamenco rhythms. Manolete, a great Gypsy dancer who was a native of Grenada, was one of the few who took his children to school. Manolete was like an uncle to me and took me under his wing. I often saw him from the window of my room in Madrid, making his way toward the Amor de Dios Dance Studio. Manolete had the feline gait of a black panther. He did not know how to write, but when he danced, the viewers were transported by the elegant sounds of his *zapateo* (cadence of his feet). I also lived with the family of the great dancer Juan Ramirez, near Benidorm, at the home of one of his brothers. There were ten brothers in all. When evening fell, at sunset, we went to Benidorm Castle, located on top of a hill, and there we gathered around in a circle while one of the brothers played guitar and another sang. All the rest of us would strike our palmas while Juan danced for *Bulerías*.* They each took turns dancing. An incredible energy and force came out of these evening get-togethers. It was a party that was tirelessly renewed.

Because I was a woman as well as a friend of Juan, I had been told never to look any of his brothers in the eye. Gazing is considered to be a form of seduction. In fact, I hardly spoke, because the brothers would ask me questions through Juan. I would not have wanted to live this way indefinitely, but because of this, I was able to continue refining my language of perceptions—telepathy—receiving all and understanding all without words, feeling others, and putting myself in others' places.

---

*[Bulerías is a fast flamenco rhythm in twelve beats. —*Ed.*]

10

We Are Not Alone

He who sees the unity of life sees himself in all living beings,
sees all living beings inside himself, and looks at everything
with an impartial eye.

BUDDHA

I would often find myself thinking about the wisdom of King Solomon. Perhaps I wanted a bit of this wisdom. Perhaps he knew how to go inside all things and to become one with the Great All. Without the wisdom of King Solomon, we are always separate and always alone.

In a store in Chinatown (in Los Angeles), I spotted a tortoise knocking his head nonstop against the glass wall of a small vivarium. It seemed that he did not realize that he was surrounded by a pane of glass rather than something through which he could cross. I asked to look at him and took him into my hands. He poked his head out of his shell and studied me. It was love at first sight. I told him: "Come, I'll take you out of here!" I named him Samson, because I wanted him to be strong forever and live eternally. It is common knowledge that turtles do live a very long time!

I loved him. He fit into the palm of my hand, and I loved caressing his beautiful shell and the top of his head. When I gently caressed his head with my index finger, he shut his little black eyes in such a way that it reminded me of all the wisdom and knowledge of King Solomon. We communicated not with words but with our hearts. I built him a splendid and large palace in my garden behind the house, and it had gardens of its own, little lakes for bathing, trays of sand, little trees, and shelters to provide protection from the sun. I tried to make a reproduction of the Alhambra for tortoises. I wanted him to be safe from wild animals. The palace was immense—and he was even free to leave if he so desired, but he stayed for my sake.

One particular day the heat was torrid. I went to Samson's palace and looked for him. He seemed sluggish and had a downcast, exhausted air about him. When he saw me, he poked his little head from his shell, raised it quite high, and stared me straight in the eyes. Never before had he looked at me with such intensity. Inside my heart, I clearly felt the sensation: "I love you." A sweet, fluid honey expanded throughout my entire being, and I slipped within the liquid shadow of his eyes, wishing to remain there. I wanted to remain eternally in this serene love.

Nevertheless, we broke apart, and I told him: "Wait, it's hot. I'm going to the house to get you some cold water." While heading to the kitchen, I thought: "I love you, too." After fetching the water, I ran back to the palace, over ground that burned my feet. In my haste I spilled half the saucer of water.

Samson was still there, dozing—but he was now asleep forever beneath the torrid noon heat in the California desert. I froze, the water from the saucer flowing over my fingers and my bare feet and the oppressive heat beating down, intolerably, upon my head. There was no longer anything in his eyes. All that sweet liquid had evaporated, and his strength had left for good. I gave the turtle the name Samson, but I had forgotten that the fate of the biblical character was to lose his strength. I did not weep. All my tears were spilling inside. I was alone and separated from the Great All. I was alone with my heart in the desert.

೪

Nunca mas vas a estar sola (You will never be alone again). These are
the words I heard from the doctors—the healers known as the doctors of heaven. This is no fairy tale. During a period in my career as
a dancer, I was hardly able to walk. It was impossible for me to dance
or even climb onto the stage. My left knee was in a very bad way. I had
seen the greatest specialist of sports arthroscopic surgery in the United
States. He advised me to give up any hope of ever dancing again and to
find something new to do with my time. Amid his talk of the meniscus, cartilage, and tendons, he said to me: "Find a new profession." A
surgical operation would have minimal results at best and might even
aggravate the injury, making it worse than before. I asked him, "What
do you mean by 'Worse than before'? That I'll never dance again?" He
said again, sententiously, "It would be better for you to start looking for
another profession."

Yet I had to dance. I had already heard a similar pronouncement
when, at fifteen, I was told that I would never dance again because of
my knees. Thanks to physical rehabilitation, I recovered full use of them
and was able to continue dancing—but I knew this time such rehabilitation was not possible. I gave dance lessons while sitting in a chair, and
I fought off pain and depression. My legs no longer held me up, and I
could collapse at any moment. For years I tried every possible remedy—
acupuncture, knee injections, and other alternative treatments—all
without any great success. After a reprieve of several months after each
treatment, the problems returned.

I failed to understand why I was having all these difficulties. In
Spain, I had practically lived in a hovel in a dilapidated neighborhood
of Madrid. Similarly, I had come close to dying following the birth of
my twins. I had survived great poverty and enormous hardships. I had
been the recipient of miracles—yet now, upon reaching the United
States, I was no longer able to dance. I felt like one of the Hebrews who
traveled through the desert with Moses—consumed by doubt despite all

the miracles. I no longer knew where to turn. What were my family and I going to live on? My children were five years old. I made my living by dancing; it was my profession. My husband was a guitarist. We worked together.

One day when I was spending time in front of a window, watching the afternoon light spill into the room, all at once, in the space of an instant, I comprehended everything. Inside I experienced a strong feeling of letting go—my entire being simply let go and I realized that I had no control. This was a revelation. All these years, I had been fighting so hard to find something so that I could continue to dance. It was as though every day a war was being waged inside me against my body. At this moment, however, I said clearly, out loud: "Great Spirit, Creator, if it is your wish that I dance, then I will dance. If not, I will do something else. I am tired of fighting. I am weary." My call was utterly sincere. I was not pretending in the hope that the Creator would heal my knee. I put myself, my entire being, into his hands. Several days later, someone told me about the doctors of heaven. I was ready to go to Mexico.

I was taken into a room and a stooped old man approached me. On closer examination, he turned out to be a man of only about twenty-eight or thirty, but he had the gait of an old man. His eyes were somewhat odd, and his voice was very soft, as if speaking was an effort for him. I could feel my heart beating furiously, and I asked myself: "What have I gotten myself into this time?" The doctor asked me to sit down on the bed, and then he asked: "What can I do for you?" In a rather shaky voice, I described my knee problem and what the American surgeons had told me. I was afraid that he could hear how hard my heart was beating, but he seemed imperturbable. Just then I felt a sensation of absolute trust—total trust such as I had never experienced before. This trust gently worked its way into all my cells. I was no longer afraid but relieved—my life was in good hands.

Over the ten years since I first met the doctors, I still have that same sensation of trust, safety, and love. The doctor looked at my knee as if he could see inside it, then he told me: "I'm going to have to operate!" He explained exactly what was taking place in my knee. He showed me the torn meniscus, the deteriorating cartilage, and the inflamed tendon. I agreed and wanted the operation. The American specialists had not wanted to operate. I knew that I was in the best possible hands.

He picked up a small scalpel. I stretched out upon the bed. There was no anesthesia, and it hurt. I closed my eyes and clenched my fists. I had the impression that someone was carving up my knee, but oddly, it was impossible even to budge my leg. After about thirty minutes, he told me: "Okay, it's done. You can get up now," I opened my eyes, expecting to see blood everywhere. Not a drop. I looked at my knee. There was only a small incision that looked like a cat scratch. He told me to stand up and walk. Nothing. No pain. I did a grand plié without pain. It was the first time in nine years that I had been able to do a grand plié!

I rested for the entire next week. My hands were burning, and my entire body felt heavy. Sometimes the lights in the house turned off or on by themselves. I could feel tickling sensations, and I often felt like laughing. One week after the operation I was dancing again. One month after, I was back on stage without experiencing any pain. Even the scratch on my knee disappeared, as if the operation had never taken place. *Nunca mas vas a estar sola* (You will never be alone again) the doctors had told me. Henceforth, my life was accompanied by the doctors of heaven. During the ten years that followed, I had five more operations for other structural problems—and all were successful.

During one of the operations I underwent in Mexico, my friend Laura, who accompanied me, saw a pair of scissors buried halfway into the nape of my neck, but I did not feel a thing. There were three doctors who took turns working, and we could see them physically—but there were many others who could not be seen, though their presence could be felt. Now their love and presence are always with me. I cannot even begin to express the gratitude and love I feel for my doctors. They never leave me. I can always feel them around me. They have supported and sustained me through some of the most difficult moments of my life, giving me guidance, help, healing, a listening ear, and advice. They have witnessed my tears and have caused me to burst out laughing. What I have learned from them and what I am still learning from them is inexpressible. They changed my entire way of looking at reality.

I often think about what they have said to me: *Vosotros os olvidais mas fácilmente de nosotros que nosotros de ustedes* (It will be easier for you to forget us than for us to forget you). *No estas sola* (You are not alone). I thank and love them.

It was at this point that my life started to change. At the very bottom of my being, I felt that I would be taking another direction—but I had no idea what it would be. During this time I was working with Adam, my husband. We performed together at large shows in some of the biggest theaters in the United States. Adam is a wonderful classical and flamenco guitarist—a musician of genius. Our performances were extremely creative in dancing and showmanship, offering new ideas, rhythms, dance steps, and theater. My brain was always working, and giving rhythm to our days was always the intense amount of practicing. It was so wonderful to be able to walk, run, dance, and pirouette without pain. It was marvelous to bring to life on the stage those choreographic visions that swirled inside my head and to be able to teach again, standing on strong legs.

My children also played musical instruments: cello and violin. Sometimes they joined us on stage. Our everyday life was rich in music, theater, review reading, passionate discussions with the *cantores* (flamenco singers) and Gypsies, lessons, rehearsals, trips . . . My head was full, and I had little time to enter into the silence.

Yet very often I would wake up in the middle of the night with the sensation of presences. The next day, however, my tumultuous life would start all over again, without leaving me time for anything else.

11

The Signs

In this universe it is love that connects everything together.
Love is the foundation of beauty and fulfillment in life.
AMMA (MATA AMRITANANDAMAYI DEVI)

There were signs. One night I dreamed of a large horse with a long mane. He seemed very old. He was a splendid, radiant creature, but he found himself trapped in something like a spider's web sculpted inside a huge crystal the size of a wall. He was unable to extricate himself from this transparent stone. Upon awakening I immediately forgot this dream. The next day I went to a small market with two friends who ran a refuge for lost animals. We had just established an association in Los Angeles for helping animals based on communication and healing.

I was in the market waiting for my friends, who were concentrating on their purchases. I had no desire to shop. This market was filled to bursting with trinkets, books, old jewelry, stuffed animals, collectibles, and various objects in copper and wood. I waited patiently in front of a stand. A blond woman wearing a blue apron was nearby. She in turn waited for someone to buy one of her trinkets. My gaze fell upon an old, dirty, blue cardboard box sitting upside down on the table. I looked at the box for a few seconds, then said to the woman: "That's a horse in a crystal." I do not know how, but I knew I was right. The words just came out of my mouth of their own accord. The woman's face paled all at once, and she looked at me, amazed, as if I had just stepped from another dimension. She picked up the box in one hand and turned it over—and there it was, the handsome horse of my dream, trapped inside a glass crystal. It was visible through the transparent plastic sheet on the front of the box. She then offered it to me. I explained my dream to her. She was filled with wonder. She confided to me that she felt that nothing was happening in her life. Everything had become drab and sad. She felt alone and depressed. The horse was like the pass of a magic wand: she thought that her life was now about to change and that this was a sign. For me it was the sign to break my own crystal and free the promise I had completely forgotten: when I was young, I had promised myself that I would help horses.

Among all the animals, horses perhaps suffer the most abuse because human beings have so much use for them. Starting from the moment when human beings began utilizing horses and giving them a commercial value, they have lost all respect for this animal. The horse was transformed into an object that had to provide a return on its investment. His mind and his feelings are secondary considerations, if they are even considered at all. How many times have I heard: "I'm going to sell that horse—he's not as valuable as I thought he would be" or "There's a problem with his health; he won't be good for anything" or "Nothing can be done with him; he's crazy." We have forgotten who horses really are and where they have come from. Now I respect my childhood promise and speak up on their behalf.

Horses can tolerate much that is incredible: hours alone in their stalls, bits, reins, spurs, riders, backaches, leg pains, fatigue, blows, insults, injuries, and so on. It is a very long list. With their physical strength, they could easily "send us packing" and "put us out to pasture," yet they accept everything we make them undergo. If the horse trade and competitions did not exist, horses, too, might find themselves on the road to extinction! Will human beings ever finally be capable of working in cooperation—in cocreation—with horses?

The horse is a great being endowed with an infinite amount of patience. Of course, all horses have different characters and temperaments. Like us, horses have different levels of sensitivity and development and varying physical capabilities. We should not try to turn someone who wants to be a pianist into a football player. The same holds true with horses: we should not impose our will upon them—but in order not to do this, we need to understand them and respect their personality; avoid constraining them; and, most important, develop with them a connection or a relationship based on mutual trust. Some have less athletic ability than others, but a greater will. Some simply suffer from stage fright and anxiety. Yet despite everything, all horses share the desire to please human beings.

It is important that a horse have the desire to collaborate with us, to give to us. "Why take by force what you can obtain through love?" asked a Powhatan chief. Love is the only key. Before riding a horse, making demands upon him, seeking his top performance, we should learn to know him, to be with him in such a way that we are truly present with him, and to forge a mind-to-mind, spirit-to-spirit connection. Only then can we apply the various techniques, knowledge, and training. All that is required of us is the honest intention to help. We all know how to communicate. It is our first language. One day, thanks to Catherine of the Three Frontiers Equicenter in Rixheim, France, I met an extraordinary man who had the most perfect, natural, and harmonious connection possible with horses. His name is Patrizio, and he is Cheyenne by origin, but he lives in Switzerland. He is often called upon to work with difficult or problem horses—those, for example, who have already sent their riders to the hospital. In very little time, in a round pen, Patrizio establishes a relationship with the horse. Although Patrizio does not appear to be doing anything special, the difficult or problem horse becomes trusting again and finds in himself a kind of awakening.

Patrizio establishes a hierarchical relationship that offers the horse the security of having a leader. He becomes the uncontested leader that the horse learns to accept, and this is how he earns the animal's trust. All of this transpires without him ever touching the horse physically. It is as if the horse was waking up to his real life for the first time. His attention is riveted on his leader, and in return, Patrizio projects his full attention on the horse. The mind of the man and the mind of the horse touch and unite. The horse trusts him and is ready to give himself entirely to Patrizio. The horse is vibrantly alive and brought back to his true essence.

When I was in Patrizio's presence I immediately felt his immense inner strength—the force of an integrated man, a free spirit. While observing his work, one of the spirit doctor's words came back to my mind: *La vida esta hecha para disfrutar* (Life is made to be in joy). This is the true goal: a collaboration with the horse, a union of minds. This was the path I wanted for my future.

12

The Awakening

I let my soul smile through my heart and my heart smile through my eyes, that I may scatter rich smiles in sad hearts.

PARAMAHANSA YOGANANDA

Several years after my encounter with the doctors, my family and I were staying in Ensenada, Mexico. While I was down there, I had the impression that something was waking up within me, like an old memory. I felt a profound connection with this Mexican land. I had not managed to speak Spanish in Mexico, accustomed as I was to Castilian Spanish—but in the air, there was a familiar feeling that I was not able to identify.

One day our host took us to visit an extremely small temple in a field that had been abandoned and left to fall into ruin. It was not at all easy to get there: we had to climb up a hill studded with stones. No one knew what purpose this temple had served. Its stone walls were collapsing. It looked more like one of the casitas where the island people of my childhood kept their animals. The field was dry, and it stretched as far as the eye could see. While I was stopped there, in the middle of this sun-soaked ground, I heard a powerful voice inside me: "It is time to begin." I realized that it was time for me to begin taking concrete steps to help animals.

Soon after, back in Los Angeles, I had a strange dream: Buried in my body in different spots were round, thick, long acupuncture needles, and an invisible hand was removing them one by one. The noise from this process was strange, because they had been lodged in me for a long time. They appeared to be made from a black lacquered wood, but I could also see that they were rusty. Each time one was removed from my body, the air entered in strongly—as if my body suddenly inhaled, as if I had just been resuscitated. I suppose these openings could have represented my chakras, but there were so many of them. In my dream I understood that the needles could not all be taken out at one time.

It all seemed so real—and I believe I still have some needles inside of me! The dream revealed that my blockages were slowly disappearing. It seemed to confirm what I had felt in Mexico: go to animals and give them help.

I began this path with my male tortoise, Samson. He was visibly ill and very weak. My dog, Calo, who was jealous of Samson, had picked him up in his mouth and had damaged his beautiful shell. My turtle suffered wounds that bled. I treated him with herbs and clay, but he was still weak. I held him in the palm of my hand. He poked out his little head, his eyes still half closed. All at once my hands began burning. Samson and I remained together like this, in perfect silence, for an hour. It seemed that time had come to a complete stop. No thoughts went through my head. He soon lifted his small head and started squirming in my hand, filled with energy. Yet I did not believe that the heat in my hands could have improved his condition.

Then there was Dulce, a small, black, three-month-old cat who had been rescued from the street, her body riddled with lead shot. Children had been having fun shooting at her. A sympathetic veterinarian had operated on her to remove from her body all the lead except for one bullet. I saw her at a shelter, half dead, lying in a cage. No one thought she would survive. In addition, she had a respiratory infection. They were planning to put her to sleep, but I said: "Please, let me try."

I took her with me and made her a small bed in my dance studio. Every time I drew near her, my hands started to burn. I held her in my hands every day. She became soft and calm, and, little by little, she began to eat and drink again. She was saved—but it took a great deal of time.

The spirit doctors always told me: *Sigue aprendiendo, sigue* (Continue to learn, continue). I did continue to learn healing techniques, and I devoured books. I tried everything, and I practiced long-distance healing as much as possible until late in the evening. Sometimes I would wake at three o'clock in the morning, still sitting in a cross-legged position, with my legs aching. I had fallen asleep while I was practicing a healing treatment!

It all felt so intangible. In dance we can work on foot technique—something concrete—but with this healing, I was unable to catch hold of anything with my fingers. It was frustrating. The greater the amount of will I put into it and the more I expected results, the less I received any results!

I visited one of the spirit doctors, who told me only: *Sigue* (Continue). I was sometimes able to help animals at the shelter where I worked as a volunteer. Then one day my dog, Calo, tore the ligament of one of his back legs at the dog park. Another dog had smashed into him while running at top speed, and I could hear his cry of pain when he hit the ground. Calo is a large rottweiler–German shepherd mix, and he is normally very stoic. Because he never complains, I knew something was wrong. After examining him the veterinarian wanted to give him anti-inflammatory medications and then operate. He told me: "I don't know if his liver can take the shock, but without surgery, he'll never walk properly again." This sentence reminded me of my own situation before I met the doctors of heaven. While waiting for the operation I started doing work on him every day. I applied every bit of knowledge I had, but I grew discouraged. It broke my heart to see him limping and trying to conceal his pain from me. It was something I knew too well from personal experience.

During this period the worst I experienced was doubt. I constantly doubted myself—so much so that I could teach courses and grant diplomas in doubt! One of the spirit doctors watched me approaching with my heart subdued, and he told me: *La duda es peor enemigo del hombre* (Doubt is man's worst enemy). *Qué te parece? Es mejor hacerlo o no?* (What do you think? Is it better to work on it or do nothing?). I felt as if I was all alone and that nothing gave me any help. Why was this so hard? He asked me: *Cuánto tiempo has tomado para aprender a bailar?* (How much time did it take you to learn how to dance?). So! Calo made progress little by little without an operation. He began walking without limping, and three months later he was frolicking like a puppy.

I had already seen what chi was all about. When I was fifteen my parents made the acquaintance of Rodrigo de Azagra, a teacher who handed down the various Albaicin techniques for controlling the life force. His family was of Chinese origin, and they had immigrated to northern Spain. This teaching had been passed down in his family from generation to generation and was similar to chi kung. All the movements that develop chi—movements of the tiger, the bear, the eagle— were based on the observation of animals. It took Rodrigo only one minute to knock down a great *kárateka,* a professional karate expert, simply by pointing his two fingers at him. This was chi.

Then I met Master Zhou. I was introduced to him by a Chinese student shortly after arriving in the United States. He was a great chi kung master who had escaped the Chinese Revolution. He had spent his life in temples, practicing chi kung with other masters, then left on foot to heal people. He was about sixty years old and did not speak English. For his healing treatments he prepared a small napkin soaked with alcohol, which was heated to 90° and was wrapped in a piece of aluminum foil. He then placed this napkin on the ailing part of the body. Next he put his left hand behind his back and waved the fingers of his right hand above the napkin—which made it burning hot! In fact, it burned so intensely that a "patient" had to yell "Hot, hot!" (it was even better in a Chinese accent) before he stopped. Yet this made him laugh! I quickly learned to say the Chinese word for hot: *"Tang, tang!"* I even saw him work on an American fireman—a strapping fellow who had come to the master while still wearing his uniform. It caused Master Zhou great amusement to burn a fireman!

I witnessed other feats he performed with chi kung: I saw him extend a thin sheet of bamboo paper in the air between two chairs, then walk on top of it—while, hanging from his arms, were two pails of water held by an incision in his flesh—without breaking the paper. I have seen a truck drive over him, stones broken on his head, a sword stuck into his neck, and other similar violence done to him—and he never was hurt. This was chi.

He took me as one of his students, and I studied chi kung with him for six months. This helped my left knee a great deal. When I went back to the sports medicine specialist, he told me he could not understand how my muscles had so reformed. He even said: "I've visited China, and I saw things there that our medicine can't explain." Unfortunately for me, I had nothing but dancing in my head, and I did not continue practicing chi kung. At that time I wasn't really interested in healing. There were great masters to take care of that.

Even before this time with Master Zhou, however, hands had been held out to me on several occasions. One day, long before this time, when I was still living in Madrid, I entered the dance studio of Pacita Tomas, with whom I was then studying, and I saw a Spanish woman who was making strange signs over the head of Pacita's husband, Joaquin. When she saw me enter the studio, with my shoes in hand, she motioned to me to come over. She looked at me intently, straight in the eyes, and told me: "You are a healer." I immediately retorted: "Ah, no I'm not. I want to dance. I don't want to be a healer." I quickly turned my back on her then and ran to the coat closet, as if I had the devil on my tail. Fate had offered me an opening to start learning, and I turned it down! I seemed to know inside that such healing would take me away from dance.

In 1992 I was asked to dance in Madrid for the commemoration of the reconciliation of the kings of Spain with the Indians of North America. This is where I met Amerindian Dhyani Ywahoo of the Cherokee people. She had been chosen to be the spokesperson for the ten tribes present. She was also working with the Dalai Lama. Her striking beauty had an aura of great wisdom. After the performance she came over to me and, looking at me through her dark eyes, told me: "You dance extremely well, but later on, you shall be a healer. Your life is going to change completely." I could sense her greatness—in her presence, I felt so much love and joy. She awoke a strange sensation in me. I was ready to follow her back to America, if only for a little while, to keep receiving this peace and wisdom. Yet I did not have time even to look in that direction—my heart, head, and feet were otherwise quite occupied. I can think only that I was extremely shortsighted.

13

When They Come into Our Lives . . .

The Wolf Savior

After the massacre by U.S. Army troops at Sand Creek, the only survivors were two women with their children. They had no food and the only tools they had were their knives. After traveling for six or seven days they decided to hide inside a burrow for the night in the middle of the forest, because the weather was extremely cold. In the middle of the night they saw a large wolf at the entrance to the burrow. They were all quite scared, but the animal just lay down peacefully and went to sleep. The next day they continued their journey and the wolf accompanied them. When they stopped to rest the oldest woman among them spoke to the wolf in the same way she would have talked to a person: "Please wolf, do something for us and our children who are famished." The wolf seemed to listen to her and kept looking at her before getting to his feet and heading toward the north. He returned late that evening with his jaws and fangs covered in blood. The women were so weak that they could barely stand, but they managed to follow him. He brought them to a buffalo carcass surrounded by a pack of wolves. None of the wolves moved a muscle. The women approached the remains, pulled out their knives and ate the pieces of meat they cut off raw. Once they felt their strength had been restored, they took more as provisions and left the carcass. At this moment the wolf pack hurled itself on the buffalo. They resumed their walk accompanied by the wolf. One night they heard steps coming near them in the snow. Just then the wolf started howling and wolves emerged from every direction to attack the intruder. The next day the eldest woman again spoke to the wolf and said: "Help us to find our tribe again." The wolf left and came back the next day to look for them. They followed him, coming to a stop at the top of a large hill. Down below they could see a Cheyenne camp set up along a river. They went down to it, but the wolf remained on the hill. The next day the woman brought him a piece of meat and told him: "You have helped us, now you can go back to your old habits." That very evening she went back to the top of the hill but the wolf was gone. This happened during the winter of 1864–1865.

A CHEYENNE LEGEND

I had a six-month-old Siamese cat that I adored. His name was Chulo (see chapter 5). Every morning, he jumped into my bed and curled around my neck. I also called him *mi ángelito* (my little angel), because he was full of light and joy. One morning when I was still in the fog of sleep, I felt as though I was communicating with his spirit. Chulo seemed quite big. I noticed that his presence seemed different from that of other days, but because I was half asleep, I did not pay much attention to this. That day, he did not come home for his breakfast. He had been run over by a car. I was devastated; I had lost my *ángelito.* I cried constantly. I went to visit the doctors of heaven. One of the spirit doctors told me: "Don't weep. Chulo is a light being who has come and gone. That is all." And he went on to say: "What do you wish?" I answered: "That he will come back to me," knowing all the while that Chulo would never return. The spirit doctor looked at me without saying a word.

Several days later I had a dream. Someone placed in my hands a small ball of silvery gray fur that was as soft as cotton—so soft that the cat did not seem real. Shortly after this I was on my way to give dance lessons north of Hollywood. That day there was not a parking place to be found. I had to park my car a long way from the dance studio. While walking toward it, I passed in front of an animal hospital I had never seen before. Outside, there was a small kitten desperately meowing in a cage. He seemed to be calling me. I knelt in front him. His fur was silvery gray with blue overtones, and he was as soft as a fluffy stuffed animal. It was the very cat I had seen in my dream! His breed is called Russian Blue. I adopted him on the spot, and of course, I was late for the dance lesson. I named him Sueno (and I also call him the king of Spain). He came into my bed every morning. He settled himself in the hollow of my stomach with his paws around my neck, and he let me use him like a cushion. He was near me during so many difficult times—a solid and comforting presence. I am convinced that he was sent to me by the doctors of heaven. He is a gift.

Sometimes animals appear in our lives without reflecting our wishes: They show up at our door, in the street, or even under the wheels of our car. It is not an act of chance if we save an animal and it stays for good in our home. I think that some animals come into our life for a reason—one that we may not always understand.

Lisa called me because a little white poodle showed up at her door. He must have run away and become lost—and not very long ago, because he seemed in good physical condition. He was absolutely insistent about entering her house. Lisa already had several cats, and she was taking care of her elderly father, who was ill. She had absolutely no intention of keeping a dog. Nevertheless, she asked me to do a communication with him.

The poodle sent me images of the family with whom he had lived before—a young girl and her mother—and he gave me to understand that he had no desire to return there, because it was his duty to be with Lisa's father. He had come for his sake. Lisa told me that since the arrival of the little dog, now baptized Tommy, her father was actually more joyful and in better health and had recovered his appetite. He also took the dog for walks, which enabled him to get out of the house a bit. Lisa began to think that she would keep Tommy if the former guardians did not show up.

But she saw posters with Tommy's photo, so she went to the address listed on them to tell them about the poodle's whereabouts. She saw a woman and a young teenage girl leaving the house. Lisa returned home, her heart wrenched. She was going through a real dilemma. Her father was extremely attached to the little poodle and was clearly doing much better—his energy was restored and he had a new desire to live. He was a new man, and Tommy seemed quite happy. Lisa gave him several opportunities to go back to his former home, leaving the door wide open, but the poodle remained glued to her father's feet and did not let go. He also had become friends with the two family cats—so, as he appeared to desire it, Lisa decided to keep him.

14

&

They Are Our Teachers

You are never alone or powerless. The force that guides the stars also guides you.

SRI ANADAMURTI

Sometimes, I believe animals come into our life only to transmit a message. It is up to us to understand them and carry out an inner change. Through communication it is quite easy to decode the message they bring. The greatest and most painful lesson I ever received, and one that later led me toward professional telepathic communication, was from Gatulina.

I had decided to live in Madrid so I could study at the famous Amor de Dios Dance Studio. The greatest artists of the flamenco world gathered there. One day a close friend, Jose Luis, brought me a kitten that he found who knows where. I lived in a small, inexpensive apartment on the eighth floor of a building in the center of Madrid, on the Gran Via. Prostitutes lived on the same floor. They were quite friendly, but the constant coming and going of men—mainly colorless businessmen who were somehow able to make themselves available in the middle of the day—was rather annoying. There were also a huge number of cockroaches in my apartment, and they had no intention of leaving. In fact, everyone in the building complained about them.

Gatulina, however, was like a light in the darkness. After her arrival the cockroaches decided to move next door to the prostitutes' apartment. It was safer there; I suspect they thought, away from the monster tiger. In every other way, too, Gatulina was the great joy of my life at that time, and I spent hours with her. I finished rehearsals earlier so that I could be with her. I did not go out. She was scrawny and suffered from rickets because of being separated from her mother too soon.

During Madrid summers no one does anything because it is deathly hot, so there were no more dance lessons. As Spaniards say: "six months of winter and six months of hell." Therefore, I decided to go to Formentera—and I brought my little cat with me, first on the bus, then on the boat. Once she settled in she adapted perfectly to life on the island, and her rickets disappeared completely. The sun replaced her lost vitamin D, and snacks of lizards and mice provided her calcium. She also found a fat old tomcat to harass. She pounced on his tail constantly. He resigned himself to accepting her constant attention: she was so charming! Gatulina was happy, and so was I. She came in every morning to wake me, and she made me laugh by bounding sideways, like a crab.

Nevertheless, September came, and I had to return to Madrid. I decided to leave my apartment near the prostitutes—it was too unhealthy, and the building had become rather dangerous. (I even had to avoid using the elevator.) It was necessary to find new lodging. My parents urged me to leave my cat behind: "Leave Gatulina here. It will be better for her. Look how happy she is, and you have your own life to live." My heart told me otherwise, but theirs was the voice of reason. We brought her to the home of Pierre, a Frenchman who lived on the island and who adored cats. My father accompanied me, because I was in tears. I did not have the strength to leave her behind. "You will always be able to visit her," the voice of reason told me. "It's not so far away." I knew full well that Gatulina had no desire to leave me, but I refused to listen to my heart. Good sense gained the upper hand. So I left her with Pierre and quickly jumped back on my bike, riding away like a thief.

Two days later, when I was in the village, someone came up to me to tell me that Gatulina had escaped and Pierre was unable to find her. Because there was no telephone or electricity on the island, I had to wait for this message to be delivered to me. My father and I went straight back to Pierre's the next day. Once I entered the garden and called her name, Gatulina came running to me. She had been hiding in the long, dry grass. Once again, despite the persistent tugging in my heart, I left her at Pierre's, because this was the most reasonable thing to do. I could come back and get her in several months. I got back on my bike, and my father said: "Don't look back!" But I did look back, and I saw that she had managed to climb up into the window and was watching me leave. She was calling to me. I turned away, my eyes filled with tears and my ears closed to her pleas. I will never forget the look on her face.

Several weeks after my return to Madrid, someone told me that Gatulina had escaped again and had never returned. I knew she must have been run over. She had surely been looking for me, but to a cat, the island must have been huge. I spent years mourning her and kicking myself for not bringing her back to Madrid. I have never completely forgiven myself. It is also for her sake that I became an animal communicator, as a way to atone and to teach others to hear their own voice and listen to their heart. When love passes close by, we should never turn our backs on it. A spirit doctor told me: *Escucha tu corazóncito* (Listen to your little heart). *Es tu corazón que te guía* (It is your heart that guides you).

A man named Pierre called me on behalf of his Icelandic bay horse, King. The horse refused to move when attempts were made to ride him. The guardian and King were very close and had an intensely intimate relationship. He had tried everything: kindness, making a fuss over King, serious conversations, threats, irritation, and force—but nothing worked, not one step. King refused to move forward, to budge even an inch. This new behavior had begun after their last ride about fifteen days earlier, and it had persisted ever since.

I communicated with King, who did not tell me much of anything.

Nothing had happened during this ride fifteen days ago. King was rather mysterious and hermetic by nature. He was remarkably intelligent, although a bit stubborn. I would have to worm information out of him if we were to learn more. I asked King if something had scared or overwhelmed him or if some event had triggered this trauma. Nothing. Not one shred of information, not one image. I stayed close to the animal and waited to hear something. The Creator, Great Spirit, knows when an animal truly needs help, and generally something is eventually transmitted to us. I enjoyed being in King's close proximity; he radiated liberty and wide-open spaces. This nonconformist attitude and inner freedom were innate qualities of this horse. Fear was completely absent in him. He inspired me.

Little by little I received bits and pieces of information: King, the stubborn Icelander, was not moving forward because Pierre was stagnating in his own life. He did not know what direction to take. King was simply reflecting Pierre's frame of mind. The most obvious aspect of this stagnation was that Pierre did not know how to assert himself in his life. He was always sweet and conciliatory—he did not know how to be firm, and he never allowed his true personality to express itself. He was, therefore, often working against his own essence. This pattern had been long established—from the time of his childhood with his mother. King was no longer budging in order to show Pierre this internal state and to force him to take the initiative and make a decision, to choose a direction. Until the time of King's refusal, when Pierre rode him, he let the horse take him wherever he thought best. Pierre had to learn to be strong and to be a leader.

When I explain to the animals' guardians what I perceive during these communications, I must have complete confidence in myself and take my courage in hand. There is a risk they may be offended, and I am never certain if what I have received as information is correct until I talk to them about it. There is also often the risk that I will make myself look completely ridiculous.

I have no love at all for looking ridiculous, but I made a promise: I gave my word always to speak the truth. This is my contract. Being a communicator means being a translator. I must be as accurate as possible—and I am not here to spy out whatever I can. Often people are worried that I discuss with their animals all their most deeply buried secrets, but this is not at all the case. I hear only what is necessary for the well-being of the animal and his guardian. Of course, I have to pay attention to the manner in which I pass along information; I must take into account people's feelings. Even the toughest and hardest individuals have delicate hearts.

People do not always realize this, but it is quite true—I have learned this truth through animals. They have shown me that every person is sensitive at the bottom, even if this sensitivity is sometimes buried quite deeply. Being a communicator means knowing how to listen to people as well as animals—and the realization that animals come into our lives to help us, to bring out qualities that are going to help us move forward in life. It is also important to know that in a communication there is no possibility of doing harm to someone. This is why King, the majestic Icelandic horse, decided the next day, after our communication, to begin moving forward when Pierre rode him. There was no longer any problem. Yet from time to time, when necessary, he would go on strike again—to remind Pierre of the lesson. King went back to moving forward, and in this way he gave Pierre a mirror for his emotions. Pierre learned quickly!

I have observed many cases similar to that of Pierre and King—that are due to an individual's inability to assert himself in life. Elsa, who worked for a senior citizen's center in Southern California, called me about her dog, Chloe. Chloe, milk chocolate in color, was a mix of several breeds and had been found abandoned at the side of the road. She had been living with Elsa for five years. Chloe would bark at and even sometimes try to attack certain people at the center—but never the same ones. Sometimes she became very aggressive if she saw them with bags or canes. Elsa was concerned and did not understand the reason behind Chloe's strange behavior. It had started about a year and a half earlier. The situation was dangerous, because all the residents of the center were elderly.

When I communicated with Chloe, I perceived the existence of a love relationship between Elsa and a man. They often seemed to be quarreling. I also saw that Elsa let herself be walked over by everyone. She was always good and kind, and she gave without rest. She had no boundaries. She also allowed herself to be criticized by the residents of the center. Chloe had assumed the role of Elsa's protector, and she prevented certain people from getting near her. She protected Elsa much as someone protects a house and garden. She guarded all the space around her guardian. I explained all this to Elsa. She admitted that the man she had been living with a year and a half earlier had been using her. She had left him and was feeling very vulnerable. She also recognized that she gave to others ceaselessly, without ever thinking about herself. She was constantly exhausted and at the end of her strength. She promised to attempt to turn over a new leaf, given that Chloe had showed her all these important points.

A woman named Ingrid called me with regard to her three-year-old dog, Polly. She was tearing to pieces everything she could get her teeth on: rugs, furniture, the wooden staircase, plants, cushions, the television remote control. Polly looked so innocent—all white with only a black patch of color over her left eye—but if people did not keep their eye on her constantly, disaster ensued. Because she had come from a shelter I thought her behavior might be the result of trauma she had suffered in her past, but I perceived nothing there—neither happy nor bad. The sensation was simply neutral. There was nothing to explain her behavior. Ingrid had many other animals, so might this behavior be caused by jealousy?

During the communication, however, Polly showed me a younger teenage boy sitting in front of a computer in his room. I felt this boy was a storehouse of much repressed emotion. She also showed me the image of a young man who seemed to appear from time to time. He would go straight to the refrigerator, then leave again. Polly did not seem to have much liking for this man.

This led me to ask Ingrid if she had any sons. As a general rule I ask in advance who is living in the house, but for some reason I had forgotten to ask this time. Ingrid also gave me a long list of the names of all the animals living in her house. She told me she was actually the mother of two boys. We discussed the problems of the youngest one, Gabriel. He had become almost autistic, but Ingrid, who constantly took care of all the animals, had not realized how serious his condition had become. Her son spent hours on end in front of the computer, shut up in his room. She and this boy lived alone with all the animals.

Her eldest son was lazy and a druggie. He came to the house only to eat and take money. Poor Ingrid was completely overwhelmed by events: she was drowning in the constant fights with the older son, her work, and all the animals to feed. Little Polly, a newcomer to this milieu, absorbed all of Gabriel's emotions and expressed them by chewing on . . . everything. I did a healing work on her that lasted several days, because Polly was a little hardheaded, and everything was restored to order. She no longer chewed on anything but her toys. Ingrid's lesson was to pay more attention to her youngest son, who had been left completely on his own. Now she could no longer ignore him.

Another woman who experienced the same kind of problem with her dog approached me during a course I was teaching. She had come to see me on the recommendation of her veterinarian. Her blue eyes were filled with worry. Her dog, Clementine, was eating everything—even the curtains on the windows—whenever she went away. She showed me photos of her house after Hurricane Clementine had passed through: There were feathers everywhere, pieces of blankets that had been ripped to shreds, and pieces of other things I was not even able to identify. Chairs were knocked over and their feet were chewed off, the remains of half-eaten objects were scattered everywhere. In short, it was a real disaster. This poor woman had recently divorced and was now working all day. She had a ten-year-old daughter and was having great difficulty making ends meet.

On her behalf I communicated with Clementine, and the first thing she showed me was how much she detested being separated from Janine, her guardian. Yet this was not enough to completely explain her extreme behavior. In the end Clementine showed me about the quarrels between the mother and daughter. These fights were frequent, and through Clementine, I could hear doors slamming, feel irritation, and see tears. There was a complete sense of chaos in this house—so complete, in fact, that I was dizzy, as if I was being sucked into a black whirlwind of emotions. Clementine also let me discover all the unease in Janine's heart: her resentment toward her ex-husband, her jealousy, her frustration, and all the accompanying emotions. I could feel all of these, but happily they remained outside of me; they were Janine's property. It was certainly much more pleasant to be on the outside than the inside here. Yet these were all feelings I recognized. I have learned to be familiar with a vast range of possible emotions: mine and those of all the other individuals with whom I've been in contact, as well as those of the animals. We all share the same feelings.

Every day I have felt these same emotions, although differently. I am amazed at how many variations there can be on the same theme. The trick is being able to choose between positive and negative emotions—this is the path to freedom. I explained to Janine that the ravages suffered in her house represented her own true inner state. All of the negative emotions were destroying her. It was time to restore order to her own internal affairs.

I happened to meet Clementine's veterinarian several months after the communication, and she told me that after this episode Janine was very grateful to her dog and decided to begin therapy. The veterinarian knew that after the communication Clementine had not destroyed the house again.

❧

I find it amazing that our outside reality so closely reflects our frame of mind. It is what we are living inside that creates our world. The spirit doctors have told me numerous times: *Tu creas tu propia realidad* (You are creating your own reality), and *Tu actitud de hoy crea tu mañana* (Your attitude today is creating your tomorrow), but still I have found it hard to believe this completely. It has taken me a long time finally to understand. It was through animals that I discovered just how true these statements are. Animals reflect our minds; they are our mirrors, they are our guides who show us how to change our interior and therefore transform our external reality.

In my work and in other environments I often experience situations that are not to my taste. At these times, I ask myself: "What in my current state is attracting this to me?" I have observed that if I am sad or negative then I either bury myself inside or become critical—and, soon enough, my state of mind has immediate echoes in my reality. As with King, who would not move, all at once everything comes to a screeching halt.

Lynley, who lived in Cincinnati, called me about her little white poodle, Audrey, who was three years old. Audrey was peeing on her cushion every night, and she did not seem to be bothered by sleeping on top of it, even when it was soaking wet. The dog was not incontinent and had no bladder problems. Also living in this house with Audrey were Lynley's husband and their thirteen-year-old son, Alex.

In my communication with Audrey it seemed to me that she dreamed about running, grew very excited, and was unable to hold back her pee. She was not even aware that she was urinating on her pillow. Along with this strange urination behavior was her great fear of going outside. This could easily have been connected to the electric fence that surrounded the yard, yet in the communication, she emphasized at length the image of the son, Alex. She showed me pictures of the boy with all his repressed rage and resentment. Every time I tried to go deeper into the communication, Audrey showed me Alex as well as the problems he was having at school. He did not seem to be accepted or appreciated by the other children. He seemed shy and closed off. She also showed me Lynley's husband. She thought he was wonderful, but he was often absent, busy with business matters.

Lynley was trying to maintain the peace and balance of this household. In speaking with her, I asked: "Is your son having a problem, by chance?" She told me: "I don't know. He never speaks to me; he plays all day on his computer." Alex shut himself in his room and would not talk. He was also suffering from psoriasis, which caused him a great deal of mental unrest, and he felt alone. Communication was nonexistent among the three occupants of this house. Only the dog, Audrey, received loving words and affection. She acted as the go-between for the three of them.

Following this communication I had to explain to Lynley that what was happening here was not at all normal and that it was time to seek help—that this would not improve on its own, that in fact the very opposite was true. Audrey had revealed this situation to me because there was good reason for her to do so. She was providing evidence of it.

Of course, sometimes there are things about which I must keep quiet. For example, while I was working on a dog that belonged to the sister of a client, the dog showed me that her guardian was eating chocolate every night in secret! The guardian's sister repeated this message, and the guardian was very vexed and unhappy that this secret had been discovered. Henceforth, I never again will open my mouth about secrets concerning chocolate!

On another occasion a cat showed me all the beer bottles lying scattered on the floor of my neighbor's apartment. This neighbor, a truck driver, had called me to treat his cat, who had been experiencing a great deal of back pain, although the examinations by the veterinarian had revealed nothing. It turned out that this man was scheduled to be admitted to the hospital himself to undergo a major back operation that was quite delicate. There was a risk that he might come out of it paralyzed. The cat was attempting to take away his pain, and he showed me the bottles so that I would understand his guardian's fear and depression—and, maybe, so that I could help him.

15

❧

Cat Gurus

Cats pretend to sleep . . . all the better to see.
FRANÇOIS RENÉ AUGUSTE DE CHATEAUBRIAND

Peggy of Los Angeles called me because her adorable four-month-old red kitten, Simba, was peeing everywhere in her apartment. I took his photo into my hands and communicated with the cat.

Simba was young and strong with a wealth of energy. He wanted to hunt. He had his fill of being locked up in the house while watching life go by outside the window. He wanted to be outside, where he could run around and climb trees. There were so many tantalizing odors out of doors! He was a warrior! Because Peggy did not understand this, Simba was peeing in the house. It was his way of expressing his discontent. I explained this to Peggy, and she decided to take the risk of allowing him to go outside. Starting on the day of his liberation, he no longer peed in the house.

Four years later, however, Peggy called me back, because now Simba was peeing on her feet every morning while she drank her coffee and on the beautiful blue drapes she had just bought and hung in the living room. I talked to Simba again and asked him what was going on. Was he unhappy? Did he need something? Why was he peeing on Peggy's feet every day? No, there was nothing wrong; everything was going just fine. In fact, everything was just great for him. It was Peggy who had the problem. He showed me what Peggy was currently going through.

"She's frustrated now and irritated. She's in love with someone who doesn't return her affection. She's sad and depressed." Simba did not know how to help her. I admit that his solution of peeing was not necessarily the ideal way of helping Peggy, but cats have their own techniques, and it is impossible to intervene. I tried to discuss this with Simba, but he kept repeating the same things to me.

I decided to ask Peggy if Simba's story was true. Was there a man in her life? Was she involved in a romantic relationship? At my questions, Peggy began weeping over the telephone. Yes, she was in love with a man, but things were not turning out as she had hoped. He did not treat her well and made fun of her. She was incapable of getting him out of her mind. This had been going on for months. I explained to her that Simba was urinating on her foot—which was a forceful manifestation—in order to bring her back to reality. Simba was telling her she should simply let go and get her life back in hand. We spoke a bit about her life and her relationships. She decided to leave this man. I then had an image of the cat: Simba was cleaning his whiskers behind her back, thinking: "This could not have happened too soon, she sure took her sweet time . . . Good riddance!"

The next morning Peggy was drinking her coffee, and for no particular reason other than affection, Simba came by and rubbed against her legs. He displayed the same behavior the next day and all the days that followed. He had his techniques, this little guru disguised as a cat.

I was called because a cat, Sandy, was urinating on an antique chair that had cost five thousand dollars. (I suppose cats believe it is far more effective in these situations to use an expensive object.) Kathleen was a psychotherapist. She brought Sandy to the veterinarian, but this provided no answers; the cat was in perfect health. Kathleen had recently married and had moved into a new house. When I looked at Sandy's photo, I told myself that he must surely be jealous of the new husband. Sandy had lived alone with Kathleen for years before this marriage.

I communicated with Sandy, a very fit gray tiger who liked to sleep on the sofas and seemed to have an attitude of complete indifference to everything. The fact is that no animal really has an indifferent attitude. Sandy was very attached to Kathleen—yet I could not perceive anything out of the ordinary. He showed me his life in the new house with Kathleen's husband, who did not get on his nerves too much. Of course, he was not very happy to see this man taking his place in the bed, but if Kathleen was happy, then he would accept it. So why was he peeing on the five-thousand-dollar chair?

Kathleen had not expressed this to anyone, but she was scared of losing her second husband as she had lost her first, and as a result, she did not share with him what she was feeling. If something was not going right, she kept it to herself. This made Sandy very ill at ease. Circumstances were no longer as they once had been—before, he had enjoyed a complete symbiosis with Kathleen. Now he could feel the tension and resentment rising inside her. Urinating on the chair was his method of transmitting to her what he felt.

The next day, I telephoned Kathleen and attempted to explain to her why her cat was urinating on her antique chair. She listened to what I had to say without offering a word. I sensed she felt a little hostile. She had no desire to be psychoanalyzed by her cat! I gave her more details and explained further why Sandy was behaving this way: it was for her sake, because he loved her. Her voice cracked a bit, and she indicated that she began to understand. She had no desire to reveal herself to me, but I felt she had grasped the situation. A month later she announced to me that Sandy was no longer peeing on the chair. She thanked me for having talked to her about it. She was going to give him back his place in the bed, and her husband was in agreement.

Margaret from San Francisco called me because her cat Kasey was using her bed as a litter box—and it was getting worse. Margaret was washing the bed linens twice a day, and she could not take it anymore. She was ready to give Kasey to an animal shelter. I asked her who was living with her. There was her daughter, another cat, and a boarder. On the spot I thought that Kasey's problematic behavior could be due to the boarder or to jealousy of the other cat. I looked at his photo on my computer screen. I closed my eyes and imprinted his image on my mind.

Next, I made a communication with Kasey, a four-year-old tiger cat. Vivacious and with a quick mind, he appeared in front of me right away. Kasey had no love for the boarder because he would not let the cat go into his room. Yet this was not reason enough to go to the bathroom on Margaret's bed! I probed deeper, asking him more questions. He talked about the relationship between Margaret and her daughter. The mother walked on eggshells around her. It seemed to me that she was angry with the younger woman, but she did not dare talk to her about it. In this communication Kasey did not tell my why, but he showed me an example of Margaret behaving toward her daughter in a way that was insincere. I did not understand all that I was seeing, because this was the sole piece of information that I received.

I was at a loss as to how to discuss this with Margaret. I started with the boarder, and next I explained to Margaret over the phone that she seemed to have some unexpressed anger toward her daughter, and it seemed to be connected to Kasey's behavior. She listened to me. There were several minutes of silence on the other end of the line, and I thought: "I must be completely mistaken . . ." Then Margaret resumed talking: her daughter was forty years old and had recently returned to live with her. She was an ex–drug addict currently in rehab.

Margaret made an effort to be friendly and to help her the best she could: she took care of her, cooked her snacks—but she was holding a great deal of anger toward her daughter, who had made such a mess of her life and was now ruining hers. Margaret knew this full well, but she did not dare to express it out of fear her daughter would feel rejected and again seek shelter in drugs. We spoke a bit longer, and she reached a decision: she would be more sincere with her daughter. I told her I would communicate with Kasey again if she would consent to keeping him. It took me several tries, because after a week of respite, he had begun making a mess on her bed again. It took us six weeks to get it right. Kasey is still living with Margaret and is behaving properly. As for the rest, Margaret has not shared that with me.

A young woman, Corinne, complained that her large tomcat, Magie, was urinating in her bedroom. Corinne was sharing a place with her future husband—and because they had to take extra large steps to get into the room without putting their foot in a pool of urine, her fiancé was not at all happy about Magie's activity. I thought that the cat was perhaps jealous of the husband-to-be, because Corinne and Magie had moved into his house and perhaps the cat was not allowed into the bedroom. Magie, however, had something else to show me.

He communicated pictures of Corinne. He showed me that she was scared to assert herself in front of her future spouse. This man seemed extremely sure of himself, very intellectual, and a little dogmatic. Corinne thought that she did not have the same mental aptitude and felt inferior to him when they had conversations. She did not dare talk to him when there were problems, and instead walked as if on eggshells. She detested confrontation and preferred the tenor to be amiable and gentle. Magie guided me to their bedroom. He showed me their lovemaking (in an image seen from afar, behind the door). It was quite passionate—which he showed me not because he was a cat voyeur, but simply to illustrate that this area of their relationship was working quite well. Nevertheless, I was a bit embarrassed.

I talked to Corinne about what I had learned from Magie. I explained that the pools of urine in front of their room had to do with her love relationship. She confessed to me that she felt intimidated in front of her future husband. She had even asked herself if he was really Mr. Right. She loved him, but she was hesitant about their future together. Yet she did not dare say anything to him. I ventured further: "In any case, everything is working out in bed!" She giggled. True enough, she told me, she had no complaints on that score. I told her that it was Magie who had shown me this. She laughed: "He's a little rascal!" Corinne felt better and made the decision to talk to her future husband about how she was feeling. She came to visit me several weeks later. The pools in front of the room had disappeared.

Anna, an actress living in Los Angeles, asked for my help for her black cat Lluna, whom she adored. Yet the cat was peeing on her new boyfriend's clothes. I had already communicated with Lluna earlier because the animal was lost. I did not need a photo; her image was engraved in my mind.

Lluna was a silky black cat, but she had a very bad character: she did not easily let people approach her. She communicated to me that there were too many men around Anna, and that she wanted to keep her for herself. She resisted the presence of this newcomer. She did not like him one bit, and she was not shy at all about showing him how she felt. Perhaps he would go away and not come back because his shirt had been soiled by her urine.

Lluna also told me that Anna was wasting her time with all these men. During the past two years many different men had passed through, and they were all nonentities. Initially, Lluna hid under the bed, then she would jump out to hiss at them and scratch and attack them—all without much success. At present she was peeing on their clothes while they were in bed with Anna. There was no way for me to discuss this behavior with Lluna—she knew exactly what she was doing, and she was quite stubborn.

Shortly afterward, Anna called to tell me that the man in question no longer interested her. Lluna had been right. A year later Anna met her future partner, but fearing Lluna's reaction, she did not dare bring him back home. Finally the day came when he had to pass the Lluna test. When the lovers entered Anna's home, Lluna headed straight for the man, looked at him, and began warmly rubbing against his legs.

❧

A male turtle, Tito, ventured into my yard and was found by my dog, Calo. Tito was the first turtle I ever had. I was enchanted by him. He became the center of attention in my family and eventually moved in to the children's room—yet he was allowed to go in and out of the house as he pleased. He sunned himself in the garden, but he never left. The other animals were not very happy about the presence of this intruder. Calo considered Tito his property because he had found him. He picked up the turtle with his mouth whenever the mood struck him. Poor little Tito would pull in his head and wait for this black monster with the black fangs to drop him abruptly whenever a squirrel caught his eye.

Noche, my black cat, was especially displeased with Tito. Caught in the claws of jealousy, she slid through the half-open door of the children's room one day at dawn and peed all over the turtle. The unfortunate Tito speedily whipped his head back into his shell and tolerated this unexpected shower with resignation. I had to scrub him with soap. Despite all this, he remained with us for several months. One fine day, though, he decided it was time to continue his life and try his chances elsewhere. He left us slowly but surely, the same way he had arrived. I sent my blessings on his path and thanked him for having shared his small and wise life with us.

16

❧

They Explain Who We Are

There are very beautiful and very savage forces in us.
ST. FRANCIS OF ASSISI

Animals feel everything. They are veritable sponges, absorbing everything that is in us on our behalf. They have access to our deepest feelings and express them in a different way. Yet we should not panic and blame ourselves if our animal is sick. This is a common and normal reaction. Often such a situation gives us the opportunity to comprehend something of importance. Though I do not know this with absolute certainty, I have noticed this effect numerous times.

I have worked with veterinarians in both the United States and Europe and have asked each of them the same question: "Do you think that animals take onto themselves the stress and concerns of their guardians—that they absorb these troubles?" All these animal professionals agree: they have noticed a correlation between an animal's mental and physical state and the state of his emotions. Often, though, this is not something they can explain to their clients. Yet several veterinarians have taken my animal communication courses, and I have been pleasantly surprised by their increased intuition, sensitivity, and perception. Perhaps in the future, taking these courses will become common practice.

Diane asked me to make a communication with her dog, Red, a female German shepherd who was suffering from persistent diarrhea. Veterinarians had not been able to help her. The poor dog was no longer sleeping at night, and neither was the family. I asked Diane to tell me about the other people living in the house. These included Diane's adolescent daughter, Melanie, and her husband.

I communicated with Red, who was simple, gentle, and faithful. She showed me more images of Melanie than anyone else in the home. I felt the unhappiness of the teenage girl. She was having problems at school. She was shy and introverted. It seemed that the other children did not accept her—and in fact rejected her because she did not fit in. I did not at all grasp what connection this could have to the dog's diarrhea, but because this was all I could see, I called Diane. I tried to explain to her that, somehow, Red's diarrhea seemed to be linked to her daughter. I passed along to her what I had felt from Red concerning Melanie.

Diane's voice broke on the other end of the line. She told me that her daughter was deaf and mute and was having problems at school. Perhaps Red was absorbing her stress. Perhaps in this way he was trying to point out something. We decided to do a session with Melanie. I met her in a stable, because she loved horses. She felt that when she was with them, she was understood.

Melanie had large eyes and was as slender and sensitive as a gazelle. I could feel she was intelligent and quite mature for her age. She had already understood many aspects of life. We sat down together in the tack room, and the horses around us were very conscious of our presence. They surrounded us with their heat, their odor, and their strength. Diane translated Melanie's sign language for me.

Several months later I saw Melanie again, and this time she was simply radiant and more self-confident. Even her way of holding herself had changed. School was going better, she continued to go horseback riding, and Red was not having diarrhea anymore. Had Red been having a physical problem whose cause was difficult to track down or had he been expressing Melanie's frame of mind?

A woman named Shelbi called me for her cat, Rom, who had a sarcoma. She wanted to know how he was feeling.

Rom was a handsome and very noble feline with a soothing and wise presence. He knew he was ill and that he did not have much longer to live, but through communication he showed me that Shelbi had lost all desire to live. She had long been feeling this way and had been trapped in a lasting depression. She was staying for him and he was staying for her, to help her keep living. Yet now it was time for him to leave; he could not stay any longer. It was also time, then, for Shelbi to make a decision.

I spoke with her and learned she worked as a nurse. She saw people dying every day, and she had lost all her taste for living. Only Rom gave her any joy. If he died, she did not know how she could survive without him. I explained to her that it was impossible to go on this way. The cat was ready and would not remain here much longer. Shelbi told me that she had considered all of that. She called me several days later. She was going to give it a shot; she made the choice to go on living. She accepted Rom's death, knowing that it was his time. In fact, his imminent death allowed her to open up to life.

I made the acquaintance of a cat named Garnet, a fourteen-year-old calico who lived with Petra in northern California. Garnet was suffering from hyperthyroidism and cancer. She had also been shot seven years earlier and remained paralyzed on one side.

During our communication she remained discreet about herself but showed me her guardian, Petra. Garnet transmitted to me that she felt very tired and ill, but that she planned to stay and do all she could for Petra. She passed on to me that her guardian was also ill, quite alone, and had huge quarrels with her family and nursed a great deal of resentment toward them. Garnet made clear that she was going to do all in her power to help Petra get through all this. I saw that she was the one and only being in Petra's life. Her guardian had no one else. Garnet told me that she would depart in peace when Petra was doing better.

After the communication Petra explained that she had cancer eleven years earlier and that it had come back three years ago. She was quite angry with her family, and she felt very alone and depressed. Yet she felt great gratitude for having Garnet in her life and was so happy that the cat loved and supported her all the time. Life was sweeter, thanks to Garnet.

I did a communication for a young woman named Claire. She told me that her female dog, Blanche, refused to let any male dogs mount her although Claire really wanted Blanche to have puppies. She could not understand why her dog, even in heat, refused all the advances from her male dog suitors. Generally speaking, dogs don't play hard to get!

When I communicated with Blanche, I could, in fact, feel that she was refusing to be bred. It was pointless for male dogs even to try! As the communication progressed, however, I saw that all her life Claire had difficulties with her sexuality as well as problems connected to her mother and childhood. As a result she was terrified of becoming pregnant and having a child. She refused her femininity, preferring to remain something of a tomboy. So Blanche also refused to have any litters.

In one of my workshops Sarah spoke of her eight-year-old chestnut mare, Sugar. The horse had nodules in her throat and fairly serious skin problems around her fetlocks. Sugar had belonged to Sarah for three years and already had the nodules when Sarah bought her. During the course of the workshop I was astonished to see that no one heard Sarah when she spoke. She had a voice that did not carry. When she spoke up everyone said: "Please talk louder. We can't hear you." In addition, every time it was her turn to speak, people did not listen to her. It was as if she was not present at all. This was odd, because to me the group had seemed very pleasant and united. Sarah herself had gentle and harmonious manners—which made the situation stranger still.

As I have mentioned here, I have often noticed that we can attract an animal who has a particular problem, which reflects an emotional difficulty we are experiencing. While making the communication with Sugar, the mare wanted primarily to show me the discomfort in her legs. The nodules did not seem to bother her. Yet I heard these words: "Talk to her about her father"—and they did not come from Sugar but from somewhere else. After the workshop I asked Sarah to talk about her relationship with her father. She admitted to me that he was extremely authoritarian and that she had never dared speak in his presence. Instead, she just swallowed her words. Further, this behavior permanently affected all areas of her life, including work and relationships with friends. She rarely said anything and, most significant, she never said no. At her job, if it was necessary to work late into the evening, she did so without complaining. If she had to do a favor for a friend at an inopportune moment, she would do it. She was smothering her own voice. Perhaps this was what Sugar had come to show her.

If an animal introduces himself to us with a certain problem, it is in order to reveal something to us until we come to identify our own difficulties. Sometimes we fail to understand, and in these instances, the animal's problem continues. Other times the problem can be repeated by another animal present in our life. We should always look inside ourselves and monitor what is happening within. The outside world reflects our inner world. Of course, animals also have their own lives that they lead for themselves.

I made a communication for a stable hand. She was a member of an international jumping team, and her horse was refusing to go forward, although she had tried everything.

He was often left alone because she frequently traveled to various competitions. He knew that at such times, his guardian's attention was directed at others. At the same time, he told me, she was having conflicts with her boyfriend, and it was high time they were resolved. The stable hand was suffering from intestinal problems due to the stress this situation caused.

I endeavored to explain in detail to the stable hand all the aspects of her relationship with her boyfriend that, during my communication, I had perceived as troubling the horse. Together, we tried to come up with solutions.

Horses are truly masters of revelation. Sometimes an emotional problem we are experiencing need only come to the surface—into our awareness—to be resolved. Other times, a great deal of talking is required. When we engage in such awareness and talking on the part of an animal we love—especially a horse—our heart will open and we can become more attentive. It was amazing to me to learn that horses also refused to budge.

I thought only donkeys acted this way!

When I was little and still living on the island of Formentera, we sometimes spent the day at Manuela's sister's house. I loved to go there—it was always an adventure! The only thing I did not care for: On our arrival, the *abuela* (grandmother), dressed in traditional black and straw hat, would offer us some of her homemade *sobresada* (a small spicy sausage) and a sugary liquor—*hierbas* (herbs)—which was a specialty of the island and was apparently quite good for the health. We had to choke these down or else she would be offended. In fact, we could never refuse any of the food that was offered to us—this was one of the customs of the island. I tried to spit out the hierbas and sobresada when she was not looking. I do not like eating pork.

The abuela had a very tight braid that fell down her back. For festivals she would put on a traditional black dress enlivened by a few colors. She spoke *payés,* a Catalan dialect, rather than Castilian Spanish. She and her family lived far away (to me), on the other end of the island.

When we visited they would hitch up their only donkey, Ara, and pile all the children and the sacks into a cart. The uncle sat up front and carried a riding crop. I detested this man. He was rough and cruel. To me he seemed to have achieved the heights of ugliness. Everything in him was hard. I scorned the riding crop he used to hurt the poor donkey, and he was always spouting fascist opinions that I did not understand, but I nevertheless knew it was not good to speak that way.

When we visited, I had my doubts that poor Ara would be able to go the distance. It was always oppressively hot, and the distance was quite far. I prayed to the Creator that Ara might make it to our destination without harm. If the donkey stopped, I would whisper to myself: "Please, keep going. Don't stop too long, or he'll strike you!"

Once, we passed through a magnificent forest filled with sweet-smelling pine trees. The entire island was perfumed with thyme, rosemary, grapevines, and the red earth—but I could not manage to take advantage of this beautiful landscape because I was so scared for Ara. When he halted I tried to distract the uncle as long as possible so that Ara would be able to regain his strength. I kept sending Ara all my energy. Donkeys are not really stubborn. They simply reach a point where they have had enough.

In primary school we had to write this phrase a thousand times as punishment: "I am a donkey, I am a donkey, I am a donkey, I am a donkey . . ." It was an impossible task. Some students wrote until dawn and still did not manage to finish. The entire class detested the schoolteacher who doled out such punishments that were entirely unjust. She wanted to humiliate us. We were all drowning in fear. In primary school, then, I began asking myself questions about the nature of human beings. I did not see why it was so bad to write "I am a donkey," because I loved donkeys, and, after all, it was true. I *am* a donkey—and I am a cow; I am an ant. We are all one. I wrote: "I am a donkey" two hundred fifty times. My mother was upset and went to the school to lodge a complaint. She was a straightforward and fair woman, and she knew how to stand firm against injustice. I admired her.

I do not remember much about school, because I did my best to disappear whenever I could. Another teacher had silvery blue hair. In winter she wore her gray suit and a fox fur decorated with fake eyes—two marbles—that gleamed. This carcass hung like a scarf around her neck. I wondered how this teacher's hair could be as blue as her eyes. For every spelling mistake she deducted five points, so I always received zeroes. My mother asked her: "Why five points for every mistake?"—but we could do nothing, so it was impossible for me to get a good grade. Yet I truly enjoyed French and poetry. When I read I could take refuge inside myself, as if I was on an island and no one said anything to me. The fox, meanwhile, often watched me. He knew full well that I could not help but make mistakes in my French. He never looked very happy. Sometimes flashes of lightning emerged from his eyes. Perhaps he had his fill of hanging around the neck of the woman with blue hair.

17

&

How to Forgive

The weak are incapable of ever forgiving. Forgiveness is an attribute of the strong.

MAHATMA GANDHI

Lili called me for her dog, Max, whom she absolutely adored. He was in the process of dying; his kidneys were no longer functioning. The veterinarian told her that Max had only two or three days left to live. Lili was crying so hard on the telephone that I could barely understand her. A flood of incoherent words just poured from her mouth, but through this call, I could feel all her pain, and it pierced me directly in the heart. I looked at Max's photo on my computer screen. It was a poor photo; I could not see him very clearly. He seemed to be a mix of several breeds, and some might have concluded that he hardly looked like a dog—but his essence was extraordinary.

I perceived his suffering: he was quite weak and on the brink of death—yet he was filled with wisdom and a certain grandeur. During our communication it became clear to me that before Max would die, Lili had to resolve problems she was having with her father. I was quite surprised; I had not expected to hear such an assessment. Apparently Lili had suffered a great deal of abuse in her childhood. Her father was a difficult and sometimes violent man. Her mother had not defended her, and therefore Lili was unable to forgive her either. She nursed a grudge against both of them for having spoiled her life. She felt she was incapable of finding a decent partner—all her relationships ended badly—because of the trauma she had experienced. Max transmitted to me that Lili should try to forgive her parents.

He also passed on to me that he had come to bring her joy and trust during the past three years they had spent together, and that he was there to help her—but he would not be able to stay much longer. I spoke about this with Lili. She told me that she was completely dependent upon Max's presence. She did not know how she was going to live without him. She wept. She was an actress and lived with her father, and she did not talk about her mother, who was now living in another state. Lili had suffered health problems—mainly with her kidneys and bladder—since the age of twelve. While I spoke with her she held in her arms this small, beloved animal who had just transmitted such compassionate messages to me. Two minutes before Max's death, the flame of the candle went out. She had the sensation of a feather caressing her cheek.

I met Lili again later. All of her health problems had vanished. She was lovely and svelte with shining blue eyes. She spoke again to me about Max and told me that it was thanks to him that she had found the strength to go on living. She had been very depressed and had wanted simply to let herself die because nothing was working out anymore. Then Max had come into her life, and everything changed. His immense love had sustained her and taught her how to laugh again.

Sometimes animals absorb our pain and misery. Tara, a massage therapist, called me because her cat, Argenon, had a tumor on his dorsal column. Because of this, he was no longer able to use his back legs. We performed a healing session for him, and afterward, he was once again able to climb up on the bed and the shelves where he liked to take his siestas. The tumor, however, was still there.

When I made a communication with him, this is what he transferred: "Tara asked me to remove her pain." Actually, Tara was experiencing terrible back problems that no doctor had been able to treat. She had been forced to abandon her profession. She took high doses of anti-pain medication and suffered enormously, and on numerous occasions she said while crying: "Please, Argenon, take this pain from me! I can't take it anymore!"

Without our realizing it, if we ask animals to help us, they often will. It is much better to ask help from the Creator. Argenon lived another two years in good health. Tara still has back problems.

Christie called me because her dog, Rosie, a German shepherd, was stricken with cancer. She wanted to know how the dog was actually feeling. Rosie lived in the country, in a very remote area, surrounded by horses.

While making my communication with Rosie, I saw that the house was very dark and that a heavy atmosphere weighed upon it. It gave off an aura of depression and boundless sorrow. I saw that Christie's husband was also sick, and I heard the words *abuse* and *alcohol*. I had no desire to linger there.

Later, Christie told me that she came from a family of alcoholics and had lived a very unhappy childhood. In addition, she was not happy in her marriage, but she was unable to leave her husband when he was suffering so greatly. Rosie would often lie down next to him, as if to try to take away his pain. She absorbed it, but then she either could not or would not cure herself of the illness. Perhaps this is a decision made by the Great Spirit.

I told Christie that there was nothing I could do for Rosie.

Sometimes, through communication, I enter the heart of families that are so sad, so overburdened, and have so many troubles to settle—it is as if a thick black cloud envelops their houses. Such a situation breaks my heart, but it was as if I was not given the right to touch it. When I have such a circumstance—when I do not have the right to interfere—the animals involved are always my main concern. I would like to wave a magic wand and so lighten such situations, but I have not been given this gift. It is hard to see such suffering and be unable to do anything to alleviate it. I feel utterly powerless, but I often must leave life as it is.

Perhaps it is a question of destiny. I have also met animals who are so sick that I wonder how they have been able to survive so long. A marvelous veterinarian named Corinne, whom I met in France and whom I love very much, told me one day: "It is incredible how much pain they can tolerate and how they just hold on!" Sometimes animals are complete wrecks—half in their body and half outside of it. They cling to life not for their own sake, but because their human guardian is not ready for them to leave. In the wild they would have left long ago.

A woman in a workshop showed me a photo of her black dog, Hamlet, who was eaten away with tumors. She could not accept the fact that he was going to die. The veterinarian had said he should have passed on long before, but he was still living. His diagnosis was correct—but Hamlet's spirit had decided otherwise. The woman was clinging to Hamlet—and he could not abandon her. She had placed all her emotional emptiness on the dog's ability to fill it. Her childhood had been unhappy and lonely. Now only Hamlet lived for her. He filled entirely the void in her life.

After the workshop, a communication, and a great many tears, she began to become aware of the nature of her relationship with her dog. A change took place inside of her, and three days later, Hamlet was able to free himself of his physical body.

The animals who come to us have a great responsibility. We humans think only about raising them, about teaching them to heel or roll over onto their bellies, and, most important, of forbidding them to climb onto the sofa. Yet without our knowing, they have undertaken a much grander and more difficult mission: initiating us into love, teaching us that we are not alone.

Since I have been communicating with animals, I have met so many people who are living lonely and loveless lives that I ask myself where all the love on our planet has gone and how we can explain this lack. Domestic animals have an increasingly important place in our lives. How could we live without them?

A woman named Michelle spoke to me about her horse, Polo, who had sarcoidosis on her inner thighs. Michelle did not know what to do to heal the horse. Her veterinarian did not want to carry out the usual treatment because of the location of the tumor; it was too risky.

During my communication with Polo, he showed me circumstances related to Michelle. Generally an animal gives me clues concerning his own issues, but when he sends me information about his guardian, it arouses my suspicions. Animals communicate about their guardians with much love and no judgment. Polo showed me there was a serious problem concerning a relationship between Michelle and a man.

After the communication I decided to talk to Michelle about it. She was a remarkable, highly intelligent woman—and one of great depth, which had won her the esteem of the horses. I explained to her what I had perceived, and tears began to flood her dark eyes. She told me that she was holding a great deal of resentment toward her ex-husband, who had abducted their son four years earlier. She had to live without the child and managed to see him only on rare occasions. She also had fought breast cancer several years earlier. Now Polo—a magnificent and noble being—was absorbing all of this. I could easily understand why Michelle loved him so much: he was an exceptional spirit! Eventually, through Polo, Michelle was able to become receptive to the idea of forgiveness. In fact, this meeting taught me a great deal about forgiveness—and that it often requires time.

John, a man living in Los Angeles, called me about his dog, Gladys, who had a large cancerous tumor on her haunch and another inoperable one in her heart. He had rescued her in Greece, where she had been beaten mercilessly and burned with cigarettes. He found her on the street, tied to a truck, her body covered with burn marks. To save her, he had endangered himself and then procured a passport that allowed him to bring her back with him to the United States, where she had lived happily with him for six years.

She was now dying, and I knew there was nothing I could do for her. John's very kind wife loved Gladys so much. Interestingly, during our communication, Gladys showed me the anger John felt toward his mother and brother, who always treated him unfairly and with whom he always quarreled. His mother manipulated him constantly, and this enraged him. The beautiful Greek dog took this anger inside herself, and perhaps this is what was transformed into the cancer in her heart. John had already experienced a heart attack, which almost killed him.

Along with Gladys, when he was in Greece, John had also rescued a young cat named Spring. Before her guardian came along, someone had thrown the cat against a wall for amusement, and Spring's skull had been fractured. In the United States, John was able to give her several years of happiness, but then the cat's spirit had to leave. I never saw any man who would do so much to rescue an animal and yet was holding so much of his own grief. We often carry violence and anger inside ourselves—it is important to learn how to transform them into love. Often we can do so through the infinite compassion transmitted by animals. They give us the key.

A woman with whom I previously had a session visited me to talk about her dog and horse. The horse regularly suffered from colic, and the dog suffered from stomach tumors. I looked at the photos she brought of both animals in order to establish a communication.

All I could see was the word *father* repeated several times. The woman looked at me with dismay and began to cry with deep, heavy sobs. She confided to me what she had learned about her father: when he was a soldier, he had witnessed his fellow comrades disembowel a young pregnant woman. Apparently, he had done nothing to try to save her. She was incapable of forgiving him, and the memory was too heavy for her. Perhaps this woman's animals expressed her suffering through their illnesses.

A woman, Linda, called me to treat her dog, Spice, whose hind legs and back were paralyzed. Before each treatment I did a communication so I could precisely identify her condition.

After several messages for Linda, I heard the words *sexual abuse*. It seemed to concern a period of Linda's childhood, and she was still scarred from it emotionally. I hesitated to discuss this with her; the information was too strong. As I've mentioned before, when I hear facts of this nature, I never speak of them directly. I simply ask a guardian leading questions to see what he or she might choose to share. I asked Linda if anything had happened to her in her teenage years. Linda told me that nothing had happened and that she had enjoyed a happy childhood. I did not push the matter further.

Next, I spoke with Linda's friend who had advised her to contact me. I asked this friend if she had known Linda since she was a teenager. She told me that when Linda was eighteen she had been raped after school by a group of young men—and Linda had confided in her, but she had not said a word about it to me.

Yet, when she contacted me later, Linda told me that since the treatment session Spice was doing much better. Perhaps it was necessary for Linda to ask herself the questions I posed in order finally to seek out therapy that would help her get on with her life. If she does not learn to forgive herself, I believe Spice will develop another illness.

Often it is through animals that we can examine our own emotions. Because we do not feel judged by animals, we can learn to forgive ourselves and others.

Sue had a dog, Tiaree, who was experiencing epileptic fits. It seemed apparent on meeting Sue that she was hiding a secret sorrow.

I made a communication with Tiaree: the dog seemed quite happy despite the very painful crises she had to undergo. It seemed to me that hers was a genetic problem, yet something else surfaced during our communication.

I approached the guardian gently: "Sue, you're scared to express your emotions, and you're holding a great deal of anxiety inside. I don't know why, but you fear losing control. It's not by chance that you've attracted a dog suffering from epilepsy." Sue told me that her two previous dogs had also been epileptic. She explained that when she was a young child her father had beaten her mother so severely that a part of her mother's brain had been destroyed. This was why she had so much sorrow inside. What an unhappy childhood! The little girl she used to be concluded that the expression of strong emotions—anger or any other—would engender a loss of control that could lead to the expression of extreme violence.

She had buried deep inside an extremely painful past—and her anger. She always held herself back until, eventually, she no longer felt anything and had shut the door to her sensitivity. Tiaree, however, had come into her life to show her how to heal, how to be in harmony. The epileptic fits were translations of her fear of losing self-control. Of course, this is not necessarily the case with every epileptic dog or cat, but it holds true in certain cases.

A man came to see me with his dog, Soleil, a female red Doberman. She was particularly gentle, and her eyes gleamed with a quiet, peaceful light. She was in the terminal stage of cancer—in fact, she had only a few weeks left to live, maybe a month or two at best. Mike loved Soleil more than anything. He had never felt such love for another being before. His entire heart opened when they were together. I communicated with Soleil, closing my eyes even though she was right in front of me.

Her eyes haunted me. There was something about her that words could not express—something infinitely kind. She was not feeling at all well, and she knew she would have to leave soon. She did not want to leave Mike, but the moment had come. She could stay no longer. During the course of the communication I received pieces of information from the Creator, Great Spirit, concerning Mike. He had been sexually abused in his childhood, and I could perceive the words *father* and *alcohol*. Soleil communicated to me that even after her death she would always be there for him, she would always envelop him in her love. I put down my page of notes. I began weeping in the face of all of Mike's pain that had come to the surface and because I had seen the immeasurable compassion of Soleil's mind. Mike looked at me uncomprehendingly. I spoke with him about what I had just experienced, and it was then that his tears began flowing over Soleil's red fur.

His stepfather had beaten him cruelly on a regular basis. He also beat Mike's mother. She in turn drank to drown her sorrows. Mike had led an extremely difficult life with a miserable childhood bathed in fear and suffering. At the time this occurred, I did not know people lived such lives in the United States—but I've witnessed an enormous amount of distress since then.

Mike was very humble, courteous, and gentle—an artist. He had a very advanced spiritual life and meditated regularly. He was a highly intelligent man and was capable of great introspection. He had also been in therapy for years. Yet the anger, hate, and resentment and the sense of powerlessness still lived deep inside him. Soleil had absorbed all of this for his sake, which might explain the genesis of her cancer. Mike told me that the four Dobermans he had owned before her had all died of cancer, too. They all came from different litters. Their diet was healthy and based on natural foods. They had no shots and lived in nature. Why, he wondered, had they also died?

Soleil, the most distinctive and most powerful of these Dobermans, had come into Mike's life to show him that he had to forgive, even if it was the hardest thing he ever did. He had to let go of his hate so that he could live. She had come to teach him how to love himself.

A week later I dreamed of her. She was walking toward a marvelous sunset, rich with resplendent colors. On awakening and feeling very happy, I thought, "Maybe she is going to be cured," but Mike, whom I had called on the telephone, immediately grasped the significance of the dream: "She is going to leave now . . ." Her death followed in a few hours. The day after, he asked me to communicate with her spirit. She thanked him for the beautiful white flowers. That very morning he had placed white roses at the foot of her photo.

My thoughts often turn to her and her hazel eyes flooded with light. At these times a fine, slight breeze comes to rest on my heart, reminding me to love myself as well.

18

❦

Lessons

What is Life? It is the glow of a firefly in the night, the breath of a buffalo in winter. It is the little shadow racing through the grass that vanishes at sunset.

CROWFOOT, BLACKFOOT WARRIOR

Sometimes animals come into our lives to teach us a lesson. Her name was Alba (Dawn). I had been in the United States for a year, and I still had not managed to adapt. Everything was so huge and so different from Madrid. I was scared—especially of being alone. All my dance students lived far away, and I rarely ran in to my neighbors. I concluded that I needed a dog for protection, and one day, my husband came home with one he had found in an animal shelter.

She was completely fearful and would not look me in the eye. With the help of loving care and attention, though, she gained weight and assurance, and she came to take to heart her role as my protector. In fact, she had my students totally terrorized. No one dared come into the house or even come near me. Yet I could not hold it against her; this was the reason I had asked for her to come into my life.

Her self-assurance carried over into her lack of desire to listen to me. One day when I was in the garden looking up at the magnificent blue sky, I understood all of sudden. It was the Creator—not Alba—who should be protecting me! At this moment all became quite clear and settled in my heart. I collect such understanding in hopes that one day I might be transformed (though this has yet to occur).

Because Alba caused my students to refuse to come to my house, I had to find someone else with whom she could live—a person who would not resist being adopted by Alba. When the time came for her to leave, Alba in fact seemed relieved. . . . Her last glance at me before climbing into the car that would take her to her new home said: "I knew I would not be staying here for very long. I did my best. I will not forget you." She watched me through the car window as she went off with her new guardian. I felt a twinge of guilt. Perhaps I was making a mistake.

Then, several years later, there was Shuki. His effect on me was like that of a hurricane that knocks down everything in its path. A shelter called me about a dog who refused to budge, who was crying all day, who refused to go on walks, and who never looked anyone in the eye. (He would turn away instead.) His former guardian had brought him to the shelter because she no longer knew what to do with him. He cried all the time and refused to go into her house. I agreed to take a look at him.

I arrived at the shelter and he turned his head to look at me—directly in the eye. I was the only person with whom he had established visual contact with his deep eyes. He was an eight-month-old husky and reminded me a bit of the wolf I had seen in Yellowstone. For me, it was love at first sight. I had no idea how I was going to keep him—I had other animals—but I accepted him as a lodger. That day I left him reluctantly, and once I had turned my back on him, I could not help thinking about him. His image was constantly in my head, his eyes in my eyes. I knew he was thinking about me and that he hoped to be with me.

The owner of the shelter brought him the next day. He jumped out of the vehicle in one bound, crossed the yard and courtyard without a leash, and hurled himself into my arms like a child. His aroma was wild and luxurious at the same time—it was different from that of other dogs. Yet once my other animals tried to approach him, he growled, showing his fangs. I then told him: "I love you, but you cannot stay here. They were here before you." The shelter owner was still parked, waiting with her van. After these words, he went off by himself with his tail down and his head hanging heavy. He seemed to understand everything I said. My heart was torn in two, but I knew his presence would disturb all the other animals; it was not fair to them. The following night I decided to communicate with him, to show my love and explain the terms and conditions of cohabitation at my house. We would try again once more.

The woman from the shelter brought him back the next day, and he conducted himself with great politeness toward the others. He had understood! I agreed to keep him—and during his stay in my home, we had a marvelous time together and shared some exceptional moments. He went out for walks with me without incident. He became friends with Calo—whom I called Maestro Calo del Monte—and Calo taught him all he knew. There was no need for a trainer: Shuki always listened to me. He even understood what I wanted before I opened my mouth. If a squirrel crossed our path, he would look at me, then look at the squirrel, then look back at me as if to say: "Let me go after him! I'm a hunter!" We had six months of happiness. His fur always smelled of the wild and power. He could hypnotize me and envelop me in a gentle coolness.

One day, though, I suddenly felt a pang of anxiety grip my heart. I rushed out and found Shuki with Luna, the little rabbit, dead at his feet. How was he able to get into the garage? Luna had lived with her sister Estrella in the enormous two-car garage that we set up to resemble their natural habitat. The rabbits had been given to me when they were still quite little, and each one would fit into the palm of my hand. I adored them. As they grew, they transformed into soft, plump black balls with large floppy ears. They were always mischievous, happy, lively, leaping for joy, and chewing whatever they could find to put in their mouths. They had even dug holes in the walls.

Of course, total freedom would have suited them better, but because they were already tame, they would not have had much chance of surviving outside. They destroyed everything, but this did not matter to me: I could feel how happy they were! When I entered their domain with parsley in hand, they started doing somersaults, one after the other, to show me their contentment. Luna was the leader. When I stretched out on the ground, the two rabbits amused themselves by jumping on me, then cuddling up and tickling my neck.

Now my sweet, beloved Luna was lying lifeless at my feet. There was no more spirit in her body. Shuki looked at me, surprised. This was the first time he had killed. He had smashed through the garage door. It took a long time to put myself back together and accept that my loving ball of fur was no longer with me—but Estrella never did get over it. She was alone, and she let herself wither away and die. Once I was over my shock and grief, I nevertheless still loved Shuki. It is hard to love an animal who has killed another animal that you love—but love is inexplicable, and it can be very simple or very complicated. Perhaps I had to go through this experience to truly learn unconditional love.

But then we found a dead squirrel in the garden. Shuki still had that air of surprise, but he had tasted blood, and his instinct as a predator was gaining the upper hand. He came from the wolf family after all. He started looking at my cat, Sueno, with a different eye. Chispa, my other cat, remained hidden in my son's bedroom the entire time that Shuki stayed with us. Sueno, however, thought of himself as the king of Spain. He ruled all. I soon noticed, though, that Sueno was no longer at ease and that he tried to use his charm on Shuki—to no effect. The danger was real. Day by day I could feel him growing increasingly vulnerable. In addition, Shuki was also dominating Calo, who was no longer the maestro. Shuki had taken this place. I called other communicators, and all of them told me: "Your dog is going to kill your cat."

I communicated with Shuki—Big Shuki who was very wise (as opposed to the small Shuki). I begged the big one to adjust so that the small one could remain in my life—but I met with no success.

He was not able to intervene. I therefore told Small Shuki: "I'm going to try to help, but I don't know if I'll be able." He understood. He wanted to do everything he could to stay with me. I called specialists and trainers. All of them told me the same thing: "If he has tasted blood, it's too late." As a last resort, I asked one of the spirit doctors. He answered me: "There is a strong likelihood that he will kill your cat. It's a risk." He never said anything lightly, and I knew inside that Sueno would not escape—so I had to separate from the dog I loved most of all in the world to save the cat I adored. I gave him to another family, who disappeared without leaving me a forwarding address. I never saw him again. I know that he has since moved on to another dimension, because I have felt his spirit several times as well as his wild fur against my body. *La vida es mas sencilla que fácil,* the spirit doctors often tell me: Life is simpler than it is easy.

19

❧

To Love

Listen, my brothers: he who understands, loves.

KABIR

Animals demonstrate the strength of unconditional love. In fact, I think we are supposed to learn it through them. I am always amazed by the tactfulness and absolute loyalty that animals show their guardians. For some, animals are the sole source of love they have in their lives, and the animals give them their all. Animals' behavior in these circumstances always reminds me of a story I read when I was little about the girl with the golden brain. Out of her desire to help, she gave a small piece of her brain to everyone who asked until she had nothing left but a drop of blood, and she died with this drop of blood on her finger.

Cheryl called me from Texas about her dog, thirteen-year-old Grace, who had just gone through a cardiac crisis. The heart attack had left her without strength and paralyzed on the floor of their trailer. Cheryl told me that Grace would not get up, and if she didn't improve she would have to be put to sleep. Because she herself was elderly, Cheryl could not lift her. She asked if I could do a treatment.

I communicated with Grace to learn her condition for myself. A large black shepherd, she was very weary and out of breath, and her head leaned to one side as if it had been twisted. Though she was exhausted, she was desperately trying to get up again, but her back paws would not move. It was as if they were dead. "I absolutely have to get up again. I need to stay." She was very aware that if she did not get back up, Cheryl would have to give the okay to put her to sleep; the veterinarian who had come had said so in Grace's presence. There was nothing else to be done, he said. Euthanasia was the only recourse. Grace had tried with all her might to communicate to the veterinarian that she did not want to leave Cheryl alone, but he had not caught on to her resistance. She looked him straight in the eyes, but he had turned away and, without a word, had left. It was painful for him to see her in this condition. Perhaps he also had a fear of death.

I spoke with Cheryl while she was sitting next to Grace. I explained to her that her dog wished to remain with her at any price. I would try to treat her, but it would take three days. Cheryl consented, but she did not appear to have much faith that it would have any positive results. I worked on Grace until late into the night. The next day Cheryl called me: Grace had risen! She was having some pain, but she was walking! I continued working on her. In a very short time she was walking pain-free, her head returned to its rightful position, and she could even run. This was no miracle result based on my powers. Grace was simply not ready to leave. Her hour had not yet come, and her spirit had made a choice: she wanted to stay with Cheryl. Was it energy or divine intervention?

As Grace recovered I spoke with Cheryl at length. She told me about her entire childhood and youth until she had escaped from her surroundings at the age of fifteen. She had been the victim of Satanic abuses perpetuated by her family—sexual horrors, torture—and has never gone back to her childhood home. I had a hard time believing such things were possible. She was trying to forget, however, and told me it was a good idea not to talk more about the subject.

Whether or not I fully understood the truth, these experiences were her reality from which she had suffered greatly. I had done all that was in my power to do. Grace was there at her side and was always present for her, alleviating her solitude and painful memories. Cheryl told me that she would never have survived without her dog. Today, two years later, Grace is still in good health. Cheryl still sends me e-mails with news about Grace.

I met a black-and-white twenty-five-year-old cat named Duncan, and this scrawny feline was fiercely determined to remain on this earth because his guardian, Karen, was extremely ill. As for him, he was in perfect health for his great age—he never even had arthritis. The only effects of age were that he was a bit slower in getting around, and he no longer jumped up on the table. Karen was a singer in Hollywood who had contracted a particular form of sclerosis several years before I met her. This affliction caused her more and more suffering, and she was very emotionally tormented, because she had had a difficult childhood and experienced very abusive relationships.

She lived alone, and this solitude was also a source of pain for her. Everyone left her because she had a difficult personality. In fact, no one could stand her. She went from one therapist to another, never experiencing any success. Doctors bombarded her with medications. She had participated in all kinds of workshops, therapies, and courses, but nothing seemed to work. Everyone had abandoned her except Duncan. He remained her only therapist and life preserver. He watched over her, protected her, and guaranteed her his ever-renewed support. In fact, thanks to Duncan she was eventually able to overcome all of this. As Mother Teresa said: "You do not have to be extraordinary to love. You just have to love without ever tiring."

A woman named Stacey called me from Philadelphia. She was extremely angry: she had bought a small, pretty three-month-old puppy, Beany, to give her love, and the dog had bitten and attacked her. Stacey already had trainers work with Beany but with no success. The dog was unpredictable and was becoming more and more aggressive, and Stacey was beginning to be scared of her. I looked at her photo. Stacey's story was hard to believe; Beany looked so adorable!

I communicated with Beany and found that she did not know why she could not manage to control herself. Although she respected Stacey, this urge would suddenly take hold of her. Then, she would bare her fangs and hurl herself on Stacey's hand. Maybe it was a nervous problem. At any rate, it did not seem that much could be done about the situation.

I gleaned from the Creator, Great Spirit, however, that Stacey came from a family that had mistreated and neglected her, and therefore she felt irremediably alone and made no efforts to develop any kind of relationship with a man. Her isolation was a safe haven. Stacey was looking for love from the little dog instead of a man. I spoke with Stacey and found out that she had in fact come from a very large family and that her childhood had been quite unhappy. She always felt rejected and lonely, and she had not had a relationship with a man for a very long time. She no longer even tried. All she asked from life was a little love and warmth, yet she had never felt important, valued, or loved.

And now, small Beany, a dog whom she loved, was baring her fangs at her. Now Stacey was scared that Beany would leap for her throat and maybe seriously injure her. I explained to her that this love, however it came, would be something she needed to learn how to find in people as well, not only in the dog. She also had to learn to give love freely while expecting nothing in return. What occurred between her and the dog was not merely happening by chance. Even if she decided not to keep Beany, perhaps she should try to learn the nature of love. Mother Teresa describes it as a paradox. She says that by loving until it hurts, there is no more pain—only more love. Perhaps this was the reason that Stacey had received a dog such as Beany. Stacy replied that she did not even know what love was; it was not something she had ever felt in her life. This was the reason why she had bought Beany.

One of my clients, Maria, had a small twelve-year-old black dog named Brazil who she had picked up who knows where. He was not the handsomest of dogs, but she adored him. Yet he urinated in the house—especially in the presence of Maria's husband. Antonio was a fine-looking man, but he took drugs, drank, and never worked. His wife took complete care of him. She lived with him and his daughter, who had been born in one of his previous relationships. Antonio, an extremely choleric and violent individual, insulted the daughter regularly and went through fits. Maria explained to me that on nights of the full moon, he would go crazy, and it was better not to be around him then. She insisted he changed into a werewolf! I could not understand why she stayed with him, but she told me she still loved him.

Her house became a living hell, and even Antonio's daughter suffered the consequences. Maria had gained a great deal of weight during the last five years of her marriage and was losing her hair. As a result, she felt ugly and unattractive. It was only when Brazil started urinating everywhere that she began to realize what had become of her life, what she had made of it. She had to relearn everything—first and foremost how to love and respect herself and how to look at herself through Brazil's love-filled eyes. Starting from the time Brazil began urinating in the house, Maria began to introduce changes into her life.

She decided that Antonio's abusive love was no longer valid for her and that she was finished with living this way. I saw her again several months later, and she was much calmer and more radiant. She told me that Brazil had died and Antonio had found a job and was soon going to leave. She now respected herself and would not let others take advantage of her.

For many people an animal often becomes the sole possibility for knowing love. For them, love exists nowhere else. Because of this they focus all they have on the animal, but one day, when the animal dies, these people again feel empty and alone. To sustain love, they have to acquire another animal right away. What they fear most of all is to find themselves without this source of affection—but such love is located inside all of us, inside all beings. Once we realize that it is present within us, it is possible to feel it. It surrounds us like a soft and comforting cloud of light that dispels all fear. Then we no longer have any need to be looking outside of ourselves, no longer any need to surround ourselves with many animals. Love is always within us. This is what we need to discover.

20

&

When We Think We Have Been Parted

To be unwanted, unloved, neglected, and forgotten by everyone, I believe that this is a poverty far greater than that in which there is nothing to eat.

MOTHER TERESA

Fear is almost palpable in animals. Most often it is due to past traumas. Sometimes it seems unfounded to us, or at the least we remain ignorant of its cause.

I communicated with a parrot named Brutus. His guardian, Lili, who lived on the East Coast, had called me because Brutus was scared of everything. He was forty-five years old. I do not know where she adopted him, but he had spent his entire life in a cage so small that he no longer knew how to use his limbs. Whenever Lili brought her hand near to take him out, he grew hysterical and started emitting parrot screams and frantically beating his wings.

Brutus was completely traumatized. I had to work on him on every level: physical, mental, and emotional. Yet thanks to these sessions and the infinite patience and steadfast love of Lili, he was able to recover the use of his limbs and became an agile parrot again. When he was finally able to move around again freely, he even became mischievous, and he cuddled with his guardian. Lili had also experienced a loveless past, a sensation of being restricted and alone, as if she was in a cage. Perhaps Brutus was a reflection of her life. By opening his cage and giving him his freedom, and by healing him with her love, she healed herself as well.

A woman, Mary, called me about her dog, Slushy, a small Lhasa Apso around four and a half years old. Whenever Mary left the house, the dog went crazy: he cried, barked, moaned, and spun around in circles. In short, he made such a scene that she often returned home in short order. She told me over the phone: "This makes four years now that I have not been going out! I'm no longer able to go anywhere." Perhaps this was a bit exaggerated? I knew, though, that Mary brought Slushy everywhere—to work, on commissions . . . She never left him.

I made a communication with Slushy, and he showed me the customary things in this situation: He felt anxiety at the idea of separation, anxiety about being all alone. Fear and panic ate at him; then came despair; and, finally, exhaustion, when he felt that all his limbs were weak. I could feel his anxiety in my own stomach; I was shut up with him in the apartment's four walls. I was shivering all over. Yet I felt there was something troubling him besides this problem. So, after waiting patiently during the course of the communication, this is what I perceived:* "Problems in her relationships with men. Ask her! But also problems in her relationship with her mother and father." I transmitted this to Mary and asked her to give some thought to the matter—there had to be something else besides separation anxiety behind Slushy's behavior.

The next day, she told me that her father never approved of any

---

*Information on the personal life of the guardian is not "told" to me by the animal. I perceive or hear it from another source in order to help the animal and its guardian.

of her relationships. The men she introduced to him were never tall enough! A good husband had to be tall—six feet at minimum. This was a strange criterion on her father's part. No one was ever good enough for his daughter. Her mother only agreed with her father. In fact, he showered all his love on his "perfect" daughter because his relationship with his wife was not good. Mary confessed to me that it had been ten years since she had a relationship. All of a sudden, then, a light went on in my head. Of course! Slushy was playing his role perfectly! He prevented Mary from going out so that she would not be able to meet a man and thus would not be able to bring him home to meet her father, who would never accept him.

Mary told me this made a great deal of sense to her. She had often wondered why Slushy did not make a scene when she left him at her parents' house and the three of them went out. Realizing she was at the end of her rope, we decided that she would put Slushy on a "vacation" for two weeks and would take advantage of Slushy's time off to go out and meet people. After one week she already felt lighter and more free. Two weeks later Slushy returned home, and there were no more scenes when Mary went out. Slushy watched her put on her coat and remained calm. I hope that since then Mary has been able to meet a man, short or tall, and been able to present him to her father.

Vivian called me from San Diego about her horse, Merlin. He was scared of everything. During rides, he would rear up and throw his riders. Once he returned to his stall, he calmed down. A veterinarian gave him a complete examination and determined he was not suffering from any problems. Vivian was ready to sell him, but the entire family loved this horse.

I made a communication with him, and he showed me terrifying shadows on his path. He saw things that were not there and immediately went into a panic. This reminded me of the sensations of fear I had felt in my childhood. While communicating with him I was terrified, and I became little again: it is night; I am scared and I hide beneath the sheets. On the island the wind is blowing and the moonlight shows the monsters coming into my room. All my limbs start trembling, and I call for help. Merlin showed me that same fear, and I tried to calm him. I tried to explain to him that what he saw did not exist, but he was still scared.

We had a number of sessions together, and he felt better. Several months later, I learned that Vivian's daughter had cancer, and that the disease had reappeared with several tumors on her spinal column. She was seventeen years old. I wondered if Merlin had absorbed the fears of the entire family, transforming them into monstrous and grotesque beings that attacked him. I asked Vivian's permission to work on her daughter as well. Many people had been praying for her already. The next day she went back to the clinic for an MRI, but no tumors appeared. The doctors thought there must have been some mistake in their previous examination. In any event, there was no more cancer. Merlin's terrors disappeared gradually over the course of his next few rides.

In lost animals we often feel fear, even terror. Obviously, when they are lost they are in a situation of total survival to which they are not at all accustomed. In the United States they must contend with the likes of cars, coyotes, or dogcatchers who try to trap them. Life in the outside world is dangerous.

A client asked my help to find a cat lost in the desert near Palm Springs. I knew there were coyotes in the neighborhood. He survived five days— and the whole time his guardian was desperately trying to find him— but a coyote finally caught him. The cat's spirit showed me the not very pleasant but rapid image of his death. I actually felt the sensation of being killed by a coyote. These animals, too, though, must eat—they are part of the natural cycle of life, but through our human eyes such a death is not peaceful.

Following my description after the communication, the poor woman returned to the desert to see if she could recover the remains of her beloved cat. Several hours later she found a handful of brown, tiger-striped fur in the brush—the same fur as that of her cat. She concluded that his spirit had come to tell us that he still existed and was doing well. She kept the tuft of fur because it represented the spirit of her cat still present and close to her.

There are some companion animals who have escaped such a death and not ended up as a feast for coyotes. In several cases I have tried to show animals the way. I've prayed, I've tried to erect barriers to protect them, but apparently I do not have the right to interfere if the hour of their death has come. Some lost animals are in such a state of shock that they seem to be dead. Sometimes they are "lost" only because they have left to explore their surroundings or they have left and have no intention of returning. Quite often they are quite bored with waiting for their guardians to return every day and are dreaming of adventure.

From the United States, with the aid of a photo, I made a communication for a cat lost in Montbéliard, France. I had been told that the cat had climbed up onto a roof, but on closer examination, I saw him climbing down a drainpipe then dashing into a narrow alley. The cat showed me a red brick building and a place where hot air was coming out of the wall. He was staying put in front of this building. He was cold and hungry, and he was not going to budge an inch. When I described the location, the husband exclaimed: "I know exactly where that is!" I told him: "Take a can of tuna with you, just in case!" The cat was there, shivering and contrite in front of the hot-air vent. He decided at this moment that cans of tuna were a better deal than leading an adventurous life out in the world.

I believe that, like snails that leave a shiny trail behind them as they pass, we leave an intangible trail behind us. This trace of a trail vibrates—and perhaps it is what remains of our past. When we touch this trail with one of our senses or with our intuition, it is as if we have touched it with a magic wand. We suddenly have access to the being who has gone away. We receive information in the form of thoughts, images, sensations, or sounds. These pieces of information help us understand. It seems to me that all these trails are like stars. They sparkle and are aware of one another. We—our stars—are parts of some whole. Physicists call this the quantum field. In this space the notion of separation no longer exists.

21

⁂

The Doorways

Once we begin developing our telepathic abilities, doors begin to open. Sometimes these are doorways to other dimensions. One night I had an amazing dream: My skin was covered with ancient hieroglyphs that I could understand. When my skin became entirely covered with these signs, it would peel away and a new skin with other hieroglyphs would appear. What was strange about this is that you could pass these signs along to others. In this dream I possessed an ancient and mystical knowledge in its entirety. When I woke up, however, I had forgotten all this knowledge!

Sometimes when we begin developing telepathic abilities, we receive odd appeals. One day I was taking part in a natural medicine workshop in which we had to perform exercises with a partner. All at once a handsome bay horse appeared between the two of us. I did not understand what he was doing there, but because the image persisted, I began listening to it: "Tell this person that she has not abandoned me and that she should stop weeping; I'm still there." Dumbfounded,

I looked at the young woman sitting in front of me and wondered if I was going crazy.

We were in the middle of Los Angeles; it went against all logic that she owned a horse. I decided to keep my mouth shut because I had no desire to appear ridiculous or to appear as one of those turbaned seers with large earrings. The horse, however, kept gently insisting, so I asked the woman if she, by any chance, owned a horse. Her eyes widened, and she answered: "Yes, but he's in Germany." I transmitted the horse's message to her, and it inspired a great flood of tears and intense emotions. This woman had left the horse she adored to try to launch an acting career in Los Angeles. She felt very guilty about leaving him behind.

I was in a restaurant when I had a vision of two cats curled up at the feet of a woman sitting at the table next to ours. It is usual in this kind of vision to perceive the animal but not really to see him. He appears more as a shadow. I pushed this vision aside and continued eating my salad. At the end of the meal I ran into this woman in the rest room. I asked if, by chance, she had one or two cats. She responded: "I have one living and one dead." I described the cat I had seen. There was no message to pass along; I was simply to pass on that both were with her.

People are always relieved when they receive a message from an animal. They are happier and content to learn their animals who have passed on are still present.

I was in a plane flying from the United States to France when the vision of a very tiny, chestnut-colored dog emerged before me. Though he was extremely endearing, I was half asleep at the end of a long journey, and I did not pay too much attention to this vision. The only idea in my head was "Get to Paris and eat a croissant." Finally, one of the women who sat next to me during the trip started talking to me. I therefore asked her if she had a little chestnut dog at home who was very young and dear and did all sorts of foolish things. I told her he seemed to be saying: "Mama, mama, come back . . ."

She recognized this description immediately, because she had just adopted him. He was still so young, and she felt very guilty for leaving him behind to take a vacation. I communicated to the little dog that his guardian would be coming home soon and not to worry.

I happened to be giving a workshop in a stable. While I was explaining the techniques of animal communication to my group of students, I had the very strong sensation that one of the horses there was calling to me, and I decided to see if I could find him during the next break. I knew that he was a very dark color and was at the back of the stable. I went from stall to stall until I found him. He was in a state of high anxiety and had to communicate. His guardians had been talking about selling him, because, apparently, he was having behavioral problems. He revealed to me his fears and anxieties, and though he did not know where he would end up, he communicated that there was a little boy who came to see him. He wanted to stay here, with the child.

After this communication the wife and child guardians convinced the husband to keep the horse.

As I have said earlier, horses react with great anxiety when they hear the word *sale* and it relates to them. We can get some idea of this if we imagine a child of seven or eight who is told that he is going to have to leave home for another place with another family. Though I am not saying that an animal is akin to an eight-year-old child, I use this example because domestic animals, like children, have no control over the decisions that are made in their regard. Parents are always the ones who decide.

When horses live in freedom they develop a group awareness; they are all united mentally and emotionally, and they react as one—even the herd's leader. A horse who has heard on countless occasions that he will be sold has clearly grasped what awaits him: he is going to lose his guardians, his security, and his companions. In addition, he wonders if he is going to be mistreated at the place where they are going to take him, and he wonders if he will be accepted or resold. He is consumed by great worries and anxiety about his future. Sometimes a horse in this situation will become aggressive, depressed, or develop colic.

Guardians then wonder why these difficulties have developed. We need to understand that on the level of basic thoughts and emotions, animals are exactly like us. They do not have a creative consciousness that allows them to build temples, superhighways, or bombs, but they do have a consciousness. In addition, they understand very well everything that is said to them as well as all the intentions behind the words. The horse is primarily an animal who takes "flight" (rather than pursues "fight") and has a highly developed sensitivity. Like a huge antenna, a horse will catch everything.

At another workshop in Los Angeles, I sat next to a woman who was a horse trainer. While she was being introduced to the other participants, a large, brown horse suddenly appeared in my field of vision. He was very agitated and strongly insistent on communicating with me. I told him: "Wait, I am trying to listen to a speaker"—it was a very intense course that required all my attention—but the horse wanted to communicate because he was not doing at all well. I told him we would communicate, but after lunch.

After the meal I established contact with him. He showed me the abuse he suffered from another trainer, his physical pain, and his solitude. Before the class resumed I spoke to the trainer who had sat next to me. Though she listened to what I said and felt very sad and responsible, she was not in a position to do much. The horse did not belong to her; it was the other trainer who took care of him. Still, she would try to do what she could.

Often, when I communicate with horses I note their great sadness and depression because they have no control over their lives. The conditions they live in are often quite hard. One condition that affects them most deeply is being imprisoned in a stall. They hate solitude. Of course, a stall may be beautiful, and it may be roomy and receive plenty of sunlight—but in the end, it is still a stall. Imagine if we were locked up inside a bathroom with only a break for one hour each day to go outside for a stroll. The bathroom may be lovely, but soon we would have our fill of looking at the splendid porcelain bathtub and the same four walls! We would rather be with our friends, outside.

There are other places where a horse must endure hardship: he may be hitched to a wall by a rope around his neck. Imagine if we were tied to a wall by the neck all day long. Imagine barely being able to eat, not being able to look over our shoulder or change position, seeing the same view all the time. These conditions rival—or are worse than—those in medieval prisons. I have heard all the reasons and justifications trainers give for such treatment. Nothing can convince me. Like us, animals are free beings. They should not be shut up in stalls or cages and should not be tied up all day. In addition, solitude is an especially terrible thing for horses and many other animals to suffer.

22

Preparation

When a man has pity on all living beings, that is the moment he becomes noble.

THE BUDDHA

In Ojai, California, I sat with Swami,* a native of Maurice Island, in the temple dedicated to Krishnamurti. It was a very warm night, and this was Swami's first visit to the United States. He always radiated an aura of kindness, peace, and love—a state that I desired to experience. At the table with us were my husband, Adam, and my children, Shaul and Enosh. It must have been about three o'clock in the morning. Suddenly I could hear barking a long way off—a single cry that was followed by the howling of coyotes. This howl abruptly plunged me into a whirlwind of space spinning in the depths of Swami's black eyes, a space of night and fear, toward the small brown dog circled by five coyotes far away in the valley.

The coyotes breathe their fetid breath on my throat. I see the yellow gleam of their eyes, their teeth, the moon in the shadows, the fear, the

---

*I hold a master's degree in comparative religions from the Sorbonne and belong to no particular religious sect or related movement.

sweat on my skin, my paws folding up beneath me, the chilly air filling my nostrils, the odor of coyote deeply permeating me inside, and the cry stopped short in my throat. Then my breath becomes the aroma exhaled by the damp earth and my sweat, and finally there is silence. This is how it is, and I am in agreement with it.

I was also in agreement with going into the depths of Swami's dark eyes, where a vast and penetrating love gently carries us toward this luminous obscurity: me, the dog, and the coyotes. Suddenly there was silence, present and infinite: the infinite silence in the breathing of my children who had become aware of the presence of death.

All beings tremble in the presence of violence. All have fear of death, and all love life. "See yourself through others," the Buddha tells us. Where do animals go after their deaths? I am told that after death there is nothingness, but even as a child I knew this was a big lie. I knew that far away, behind my thoughts and emotions, there was a deep sensation of being detached from the narrow awareness of the "me" of Laila, and I knew that she would never disappear.

When I was about ten years old on Formentera, I was present at the death of a rabbit. Manuela, the peasant woman with whom we lived, called me to come help her. I ran to the tree from where I had heard her voice coming, and there I saw a brown rabbit hanging from a branch looking at me in distress. Manuela was brandishing the only sharp knife she had in her kitchen. The blade glittered in the sunlight, just like her gold tooth. She was laughing. She put a plate in my hands. I remained frozen, bound to the eyes of the rabbit; tied to the beautiful floppy, brown ears, my legs immobilized by the sudden fear that overtook me.

All at once the blood spurted scarlet into the plate, and a warm vapor climbed into my nostrils and veiled my eyes, separating our joined gaze while the light softly went out. It became a very tiny gleam, like that of the lighthouse on Mount El Pilar that can be seen glowing through the fog at night, far away at the very end of the island. It is there to guide boats so they do not break up against the reefs. Then, when it turned, there was night, nothing more. There was only the sound of the waves and the smell of salt. Yet this was just for an instant. The other time, that of thyme, sun, and the Mediterranean, kept flowing without stopping.

I worked as a volunteer in a rescue shelter for dogs in Los Angeles. I had received several photos and questions concerning difficult cases and traumas. The moment I entered the shelter, all the animals gathered around me in the hope of finding something. Depending on how long they had been at the shelter, they were either desperate or resigned.

There was also a large black dog stretched out along the foot of a wall, sleeping. One day one of the assistants told me: "That's Daisy, she's incontinent and hasn't budged in two months. We're going to put her to sleep." I was heading toward the other building to make communications, far from the smells and constant barking, when the assistant shouted at me from behind: "All the same, pay some attention to Daisy—just to see if she responds."

There was no need of a photo for this communication. Daisy's image was in my head. Her body was heavy, weary, and sad. It was impossible for her to hold in her urine. I felt her sensation of shame and not being wanted. Love was something she did not know; she had never received any. A great deal of suffering radiated from her being. She sent me images of her past: she had been tied to a rope in the backyard all her life. Loneliness. Boredom. Nothing to do. The heat. The awful dog food. The cement beneath her paws. One tree, the dead grass. The wall of the house. There were many voices from the house—children—but no one came to see her. She was always left alone. Each day seemed to last an eternity.

Then she came to the shelter: "I would like to stay here. Let me live, let me listen to the other dogs and feel the life around me, the odors, the children, the people. I would like to stay here a little longer, even if I'm peeing on things. Please. I don't want to leave." Feeling a sharp pang in my heart, I returned to the main building of the shelter. When I opened the door, Daisy came running to me with her tail held high. She leaped up on me, her paws almost at the level of my neck, and she licked the tears from my cheeks. The assistants were shocked. This was the first time since she had come to the shelter that she had stood up like this. I had listened to her, and she had been understood. She was grateful and filled with renewed hope. I managed to convince the owners of the refuge to keep her. We took up a collection that would support feeding and lodging her for the time she had remaining to live.

In some situations an animal is ready to leave. My very special friend Robin called me to do a healing for her dog, a female collie who was seven years old and had a collapsed trachea. I went to Robin's house, and the treatment went well. The next day she told me: "I have to go shopping, I'll be back soon—just go in and give Duchess her treatment." The minute the door shut and the noise of the car engine had vanished in the distance, Duchess looked at me with a ferocious expression, baring her teeth. She was a very well-trained dog who lived up to her name. I had always known her to have good manners. Yet instantaneously she had metamorphosed into a savage beast. I spoke to her in a loud voice, cajoling her, but she growled more and more, never taking her eyes off me. Angered, I crossed my arms over my chest and asked her: "What is going on here?" She transmitted the following sensations to me: "Don't touch me; get out of here!" "But why?" I asked. "Yesterday you were in agreement with this." "That was only to please Robin. I do not want any treatments. I want to leave—just don't touch me!"

My friend came home to find us facing each other a good distance apart, never taking our eyes off each other. Duchess did not want to be a burden to Robin, who had recently lost her father after a long and painful battle with cancer. She wanted to leave in dignity, physically intact, with integrity and without shame. She did not want Robin to have to witness her physical deterioration. Duchess was a very domesticated dog who appreciated compliments and loved to be clean, to smell good, and to be brushed by Robin. She was not the kind of dog who likes to roll in the mud. She wanted Robin to remember her as beautiful and vibrant, with her fur still clear and silky, her tail still fluffy, and her eyes glowing. Robin listened to me with tears in her eyes, then she said: "Deep down, I knew this was the case." Several weeks later, without spilling a single tear, she brought Duchess to the veterinarian so he could put her to sleep. Duchess departed proudly, with class and elegance, in all her collie beauty.

I met Diane and her twelve-year-old dog, Reba, during a performance I gave north of San Francisco, in the wine region. The location was magnificent; we were outdoors in front of a lake. Diane sold tickets at the entrance, and Reba sat beneath a table. The moment I laid eyes on the dog I sensed that she was special, but because I was preparing to go on stage, I did not pay any more attention. After the performance I spoke to Diane, who asked me to do a communication with Reba, because the dog had tumors and was scheduled to have an operation a week later.

Diane, who lived alone, had become epileptic ten years earlier. In addition, she had other health issues and had difficulty moving around. Reba was a completely ordinary dog, but one day Diane realized that Reba had the ability to warn her of an epileptic seizure five minutes before it would occur. No one had ever taught her this, but when she sensed a crisis coming on, she would place her paw on Diane's arm and make a funny noise in her throat. Thanks to her, Diane was able to drive on the highway and pull off before a crisis began. Reba also helped her get out of an epileptic crisis, and she could seek aid if she saw Diane was not coming out of it.

Obviously, the two were inseparable. The love and attention they had for each other were visible, even tangible. In the communication, however, Reba transmitted to me that she had to leave; her time had come. She could not be cured. She had come to help and support Diane and to give her this great love. Several months later Diane sent me a postcard and a photo of Reba to announce her death. I do not know what became of Diane.

23

The Afterlife

*The spirit that is in all beings is also immortal. Do not
mourn the death of something that cannot die.*

BHAGAVAD GITA

Mady called me in tears because her three-month-old Siamese kitten,
Soleil, had just been run over. He had died instantly. Mady found it
terribly unfair that her little cat had been taken away from her this way,
so brutally. I communicated with Soleil's spirit (the same as communicating with a living animal). In the photo of the Siamese cat I saw
reminders of my own cat Chulo. Soleil appeared to me at once. He was
immense in my field of vision, and somewhat ethereal. His body had no
substance. Soleil communicated to me that he had come to spend a brief
time in Mady's life, to give her joy.

In this communication he was like a ray of sunlight—agile, rapid, and
playful. He showed me that Mady had a great need to learn what joy
was—she had a strict mother and an authoritarian, distant father. As a
result, Mady had led a dark and sorrowful childhood: no toys, no friends,
no bursts of laughter. Her sole breaks from this drab routine were serious
matters and obligations. Soleil had entered her life in the form of a playful
and mischievous kitten in order for Mady to know the sensation of joy.

I passed on to Mady what Soleil had transmitted to me. This message moved her greatly. Her father had been extremely hard—she was constantly punished for trifles, and, consequently, she always lived in fear. Her mother, also very strict, never gave her any support. She had lived a childhood that was based solely on discipline. Once she became an adult, nothing changed. Her entire life resembled a painting without colors. Only Soleil introduced new touches of color—and had included a palette and brushes. After hearing Soleil's message, Mady still carried the same grief, but she could accept his death more easily. He still existed; he was just somewhere else. She now realized that she contained inside her heart a vast rainbow and that it was possible for her to find joy.

Chris called me about her small, white dog, Geboy, who had died recently. When alive, he had been both deaf and blind, but he was the being she had loved most in her life.

When she returned from Montana, where she had spent two weeks of vacation, Chris was in a car accident: she had set the cruise control, but all of a sudden, her brakes had stopped working. As a result, she roared down the highway with no way to control her speed. She steered to the right to avoid a truck that was in front of her, but the car flipped over twice then hurtled down a hill. She emerged unscathed. Her large dog, Big Boy, was also unhurt, but Geboy, who had been sleeping on the seat, had vanished. The firemen arrived on the scene and found him in the same position he had been in the car, but hidden in the bushes. Geboy got up as if nothing was wrong and started running toward Chris, who was crying. She appeared fine, but the firemen said she might have a contusion or internal bleeding. Chris was forced to spend two days in the hospital under observation, but all she could think of was Geboy. Once she had been given permission to leave, she raced over to the veterinarian's, where the dogs had been housed. There she was told it would be better to euthanize Geboy in any case, because he was so old. She decided that the time had come to put him to sleep.

A week later she called me, weeping buckets and full of regret, wondering whether she had done the right thing—so I asked to communicate with the dog's spirit. I saw a dog that resembled Geboy—at least, this is how I perceived him. He appeared large, and he radiated light. I heard: "I chose this moment to leave, I love her, and thank her for the gift." I asked Chris what the gift was. Her voice choked up. After several seconds of silence at the other end of the line, she told me she had decided to bring Geboy to the mountains during their stay in Montana, to her brother's cabin, because she knew the dog did not have much time left.

Some words transmitted allow us to go beyond our doubts and know that there is life after death. Some people do not believe in the afterlife, but still they may ask me to do a communication because they cannot manage to detach themselves from their beloved animal. Often the message I receive helps them to let go, because they feel that the spirit of the animal still exists. Such a message resonates in their heart, to the depths of their being. Beyond culture, religion, and beliefs, at their very foundation they know that death does not exist.

Often a message from a departed beloved animal helps us get past the fear of what might happen to us after death, for in the Judeo-Christian tradition we have been inculcated with the notion of punishment. Even atheists are scared, because death involves the domain of the unknown. Not believing in the Creator does not remove the fear; whether or not we believe in the Creator, we may fear death. Only men and women of great faith—medicine men or saints—may experience less fear. We all have different ways of perceiving the world of the beyond, but what matters is that a message from an animal we have loved gives peace to those of us who remain behind. It allows us to go on living our lives.

It is not always necessary to go through a communication to understand what has been transmitted to us. Even without a communication an animal is going to figure out a way to pass along a message to us.

Some of us may feel the presence of our animal—hear a meow, bark, or gallop; feel a rubbing against our legs and a weight on our bed; or see crumpled sheets. We might also see the name of our animal several times in different places, or we may dream of him. Some sign—a familiar sensation—will make its way to us.

These are messages on the part of a deceased animal to show us that it still exists and that we are not alone. I am not a medium, and I do not speak with the dead; I am only an animal communicator. If I receive messages or images, it is only because an animal's spirit insists on passing a message through me from the other side of the veil.

During a trip to France, I stayed in the pretty village of Abeilhan, in the Hérailt region, with my dear friend Hélène. We had planned to meet another friend, Juan, and then wanted to visit a former nineteenth-century stable whose cellar had been transformed into a restaurant. During our visit we also met the owners of the premises. I had hardly entered the place when I felt the strong presence of horses. Hélène had a similar sensation. The owner gave us a tour of the building and showed us the former groom's lodging on the ground floor.

I had a vision of the horses. They were large, strong, and muscled bays that had worked in hitching teams. They were tied to the wall, separated from each other by a partition. It was chilly and dark. I smelled their odor, their sweat after a hard day's work, then the persistent odor of straw. My attention was drawn to the back of the room, to the right. I saw a large bay horse there accompanied by a light and supple white horse. The white horse was a kind of double who looked ethereal. I did not understand what he was doing there; he was out of place in this stable.

I suddenly felt a huge pain penetrate my belly, and I burst out sobbing. The sensation was so strong that I was unable to breathe, and I had to leave. Once more I saw the vision of the Hungarian bay in front of me. He showed me images: I saw an accident, a team on the ground, wheels off their axles, a twelve-year-old injured boy dressed in old-fashioned clothes. The Hungarian bay had blood in his eyes. Had he been beaten after this accident? His suffering seemed enormous . . . I could barely contain it.

Once I regained hold of my emotions, I returned to the room, still anxious. Hélène, who had a highly refined intuition, had seen the representation of a woman dressed in a bygone style. She felt that there was a connection between the horses and this woman who did not want to depart. We both decided to pray for them. I asked the Creator, Great Spirit, to free the Hungarian bay, and I led him toward the light.

Little by little my anxiety turned into a sense of peace. A feeling of harmony grew inside me and became a sensation as subtle as the dew. I stood up. Hélène had finished at the same time. We looked at each other and tacitly understood.

The owner told us he did not know the history of the place. A woman who seemed quite tyrannical had apparently lived there in another time, as did a white horse (who lived in this place more recently). I felt the horse might have lived there about twenty years ago. The current owner thought he might have a photo of this horse. His son came back later with an old album in which we found a photo of a limber white horse who seemed ethereal. He had lived in the stable by himself until he was quite old. Had he come to help the large bay horse?

Isabelle called me to communicate with the spirit of her mare, Djeda, whom she had greatly loved. Djeda's death had been extremely traumatic, and Isabelle felt terribly guilty. The horse had given birth to a stillborn foal that became stuck while being born. They tried to save the mare by bringing her to the clinic, but at the first curve in the road, the mare had fallen down in the truck. They had pulled her from the truck, and the veterinarian had operated on her on the ground of the parking lot, but the saw was broken and he had no others. They brought her into the operating room to give her a caesarian. She was unable to move for three days.

When she finally regained the strength to get up, she slipped on the tiled floor, severing her pelvic nerves. After intensive care, they finally managed to get her back onto her feet. Isabelle and her husband decided to bring her home, but before they got her into the van they realized that the skin around her crotch had given way, and they took her back to the clinic. Finally, the veterinarian gave them permission to take her back in the morning. The husband arrived at the clinic with the van and found Djeda dead in her stall. It was noon, and Isabelle did not have a chance to see Djeda again and say good-bye. As a result, she mourned for years and held such deep pain in her heart.

When I spoke with Djeda's spirit, I saw a resplendent horse with a rich presence full of wisdom. Djeda tried to explain to them that it was her time to leave. It seemed to me that this was the reason for the miscarriage. There were no accidents, and no one could be held responsible. She especially wanted to explain to Isabelle that there were no mistakes, that everything had followed the order of things, and, most important, she, Djeda, existed, and they would see each other again.

I visited a stable in Los Angeles, and, while speaking with the manager, Frank, I suddenly saw, behind the nape of his neck, the shadow of a horse. This horse was large and somewhat transparent, and seemed to be a dappled white—and he seemed to be chewing on Frank's hair! In my surprise, I thought: "Perhaps there is a horse here who wants to communicate." Yet because this white horse was slightly luminous and seemed not to exist in normal time, I asked Frank if he knew him. He recognized him immediately as his favorite horse from childhood who loved to chew on the hair at the back of his neck. With tears rolling down his cheeks, he explained how grateful he was to feel the horse's presence again.

That same evening I was relaxing in my bath when the same horse again appeared in my field of vision. Though my bath, fragrant with essential oils, had me floating tranquilly on the aroma of rosemary toward the island of Formentera, this horse had no intention of letting me settle into daydreams. He had messages for Frank—messages about his life. I protested that I did not make a habit of bringing a pen into the bathtub with me, but he gently insisted. At the end of our communication, overtaken by curiosity, I asked him: "Where do horses go after death?" I received these images: dazzling and immense light beings in the form of horses, existing together as a herd. They galloped in freedom, and they radiated a sensation of wisdom. After a brief instant the images were gone, but the sensation remained in my heart. The next day I passed along to Frank the message I had been given by my nocturnal visitor.

When I was staying at an Icelandic ranch in Weiterswiller, a white mare appeared to me during my daily meditations. She had a fine-shaped head and a long mane that fell to the left of her neck. I asked her to come back later, but she remained suspended between the flame of my candle and me. A beautiful golden white light radiated from her. She transmitted to me that she had come to help the other horses.

When I spoke to Ute, the owner of the ranch, she recognized the horse immediately and said: "That was Hela, the mother of Hetjia." She brought me into the forest to see Hetjia, because mother and foal resembled each other so closely. The pony was identical to the horse in my vision—except that her mane fell to the right of her neck, not the left.

24

&

When You Light
a Candle

*Every healing is essentially a liberation from fear. Fear
arises from lack of love. The only remedy for lack of love
is perfect love.*

DR. HELEN SCHUCMAN, *A COURSE IN MIRACLES*

In my practice I most prefer performing the healings, because they
require taking a communication much further. When there are emotional depths that the animal is absorbing for his guardian, however,
healings become more complicated. At these times I must also communicate with the spirit of the human involved. For me, the spirit is the
luminous part of the being that exists eternally.

In the case of my dog Shuki, as I've indicated (chapter 18), I always
saw a big Shuki and a small one. Big Shuki was very wise and philosoph-
ical and compassionate. He had so much love that arose from his spirit
that I was sometimes disappointed when I talked to Small Shuki. In
the beginning I was a little uneasy and could not understand why I was
seeing double—Big and Small Shuki in one dog. Perhaps it was a sign
that I now needed glasses? Big Shuki, somewhat intangible, was unable

to change the personality of Small Shuki, especially with regard to kill-ing prey. The killer instinct was part of Small Shuki. When I asked Big Shuki to do something, he told me that he could not intervene.

Most often, in the case of physically serious healing treatment, I ask to speak to the animal's spirit. In certain cases, it turns out that this spirit is unable to step in. There are issues concerning the recovery of an animal that do not belong to us, and because of this, there is noth-ing we can do—only the Creator heals the animal. Of course, every case is different, but I have struggled with doubts and have questioned my abilities, although I have witnessed the marvelous.

In the beginning I felt responsible for an animal's outcome, and I would work until two o'clock in the morning if necessary. Later, I real-ized that the strength of my will that had guided me in my life as a dancer was of no use now. To the contrary, I had to release my will, let go and enter a state of absolute trust. It was extremely difficult for me—because I had had no religious instruction when I was growing up, I did not grasp the notion of faith. I had always been attracted to all kinds of saints. I had read the lives of Christian saints such as John of the Cross and Teresa of Avila, Eastern yogis such as Yogananda, Muktananda, and great tsaddiks such as Isaac Luria and Shimon Bar Yochai. I had even studied the history of religions, but when I realized that for me it was only an academic exercise, I left the path of a theological degree.

In addition, all those hours spent in the library, poring over books, did not leave me any time to dance! I concluded that books are only the words of other human beings—of course, human beings that cer-tainly may be wiser and have greater knowledge, but human beings who are still subject to error and interpretation. In dance, at least, my heart vibrated, my entire being breathed, and I formed part of the whole. Academic study seemed too dry to me. I have been told that in order to teach Hebrew to children, honey must be placed on every letter. Letters are living things; they have energy and are filled with sweetness, but I do not know Hebrew, and in my theological studies I found no honey. I would find honey on another path. In my case, I wanted the love—the honey—that I saw in the eyes of Paramahansa Yogananda.

I come from a family of writers who had books on every wall of the house. I come from people of the book, and what I was looking for was not there. In dance, at the beginning I had no ambition and little discipline. I just wanted to move, to answer the need I had deep within me. It took me years of hard work to transform this desire into ambition and to attain the high level that allowed me to perform in large theaters. An artist needs a solid ego to survive in the performance world. It was the power of my will that guided me, despite my damaged knees, my fragile health, and the birth of my beautiful twins—not to mention the poverty I endured. I almost died several times. Yet the opposite is true in the world of healing treatments: we should let go of everything and submit.

La Chana had sent me to a small evangelical church near Barcelona in which members sang to the Creator and flamenco and went into a kind of religious trance. Many of them did not know how to read, but I was unable to forget the fruits of my education, which made me laugh when I heard the officiating priest mightily deliver his sermons on the spirit and hell. In truth, it became apparent that no one understood a thing about what the priest was talking about. They knew only that they were supposed to be scared because the officiating priest, who was a gadjo (non-Gypsy), pointed his finger at and fixed his threatening eye on all the Gypsies sitting in the room, shouting at them with all the power of his lungs.

Fear and threats are something with which the Gypsies are all too familiar. It forms part of their experience in the gadjo world—they are always under attack from the authorities and obliged to keep moving from place to place. I could not enter into a religious system based on fear—and why was there a need to shout in order for the Creator to hear us? This method, however, certainly worked for members of that church. Some of them, as I've said, went into a kind of ecstatic trance; others spoke in tongues. The sublime music, songs, and voices transformed all this energy into a magnificent spiritual experience. I could see that the entire group of Gypsies became one, united by their faith. This was an impressive sight, but it did not lead me to opening my heart.

When I began performing healings, I knew that this was the path of learning for me. I would discover without books. I clearly observed that my will had no effect: a healing treatment took place between the Creator and the animal. According to traditional teachings, the techniques used in such treatments raise the vibratory frequency and remove blockages. I have had to accept that not all animals will be healed. Fate and obstructive emotions may decide otherwise.

Even so, techniques involving the manipulation of energy are one thing, but results garnered from ten minutes of simple prayer or a request is something altogether different. To what do these results correspond—and why do they succeed only some of the time? I do not have these answers.

Bello, a chestnut horse, taught me perseverance and trust. Vickie called me because the horse had such bad arthritis that he was no longer able to move—though at one time he had been a champion. After his glory days, she found him in a field, alone and abandoned, thin and depressed. He no longer had any desire to live. It was a prospect that no longer interested him, and his spirit was absent. At that time he was able to come back to life only because Vickie gave him a great deal of attention and care.

When making the communication with him, I saw an extremely hurtful past: stress, steroid injections, an acidic substance placed beneath his feet that caused a painful burning sensation, acute pains in his legs, and tension. Along with all this physical pain were the nervousness and the parade of pressures, races, and imprisonments. The trainer at the stable where he lived in his time with Vickie told me that in fact for races a kind of wooden plate was placed under his front feet to lift a horse higher. This gave him style! The horse would remain for hours in this position. As for the acid under the horse's feet—apparently use of this solution is still practiced.

I began my healing on Bello from a distance. There was very little improvement, and I could not understand why. So I communicated with him again and again. I always felt a pang when I listened to him. I reached the conclusion that to him, healing meant the resumption of racing and the miserable life he had led before. This is why he preferred to suffer from arthritis. It was not a conscious decision—but it was a decision all the same. It took me weeks before he could glimpse that another future was possible.

I treated him repeatedly, did communications, offered prayers. Each time, he improved a tiny bit—and each time, we had to start all over again. I was determined not to throw in the towel. I was doing it for him and for all racehorses. I knew through my own experience when I could barely walk that the doctors of heaven had cured me and allowed me to dance again.

It took several months of working with Bello before he was free again, and I truly believe he needed all this time. We had succeeded: He could gallop like a young colt. He now enjoys full health and is living in Frank's stable. We are all very proud of him.

Sue, a young woman of Indian origin who did not live very far from me in the San Fernando Valley in Los Angeles, came to see me with Toby, her twelve-year-old little gray dog. She adored Toby; he was the love of her life. Yet he had such bad arthritis that he moved very slowly with a great deal of pain. He had been in this condition for a long time. I knew it would take time to treat him. I placed my hands on him and prayed, and he slept like an angel during this session. The next day Sue called me and said: "There's nothing wrong with him anymore! He's running like he did when he was three! He's completely healed!"

I was truly amazed; I had not expected this outcome so quickly. Sue spent the entire week going on long walks with Toby for hours at a time. She was so delighted to see him young, sparkling, and full of vitality. They even hiked up the mountain to dip their feet in the water.

The last day of the week, Toby died. He passed away in his sleep with no warning. Yet Sue could not mourn, because she remembered that wonderful week of happiness and magical moments. They shared these final, splendid moments of mutual love untroubled by sorrow and pain so that Sue could remember that love exists and that there is indeed life after death.

I will never forget Pennylane, the magnificent black mare. She is etched into my heart forever. Thanks to her I asked myself every possible question about healing treatments, fate, the Creator's intervention, the nature of our spirit, and the nature of human beings.

In September the veterinarian Johannes called me to help Pennylane, who lived in Germany. She was lying on the ground, her entire body shaking, and no one knew what to do. Her guardians wanted to put her to sleep, but Johannes was against this. She was a young horse, and he felt she could be healed. I worked on her as an emergency. Shortly after our time together, she stood up again. I next had a brief communication with her to see what she was feeling.

Pennylane had immense fear of a woman—her guardian—and the horse knew they wanted to have her put down. She wanted to live. She was not at all ready to leave. I determined that if Pennylane remained in their presence, she would suffer another crisis. Johannes therefore decided to keep her with him a bit longer while I continued working on her. What was most important during these three weeks: the love, attention, and kindness that Johannes gave Pennylane.

After this time she was completely recovered and felt fine, although she was skinny. Unfortunately, Johannes could no longer keep her, so she returned to her guardians and I had no more news of her. Several months later, however, I spoke to Johannes and asked him for news of Pennylane. He told me: "They killed her one week later." I was shocked: "Why?" "Because she was too thin," he responded. We both wept. Johannes himself died several months later—an unexpected death for all who knew him. Johannes was a remarkable veterinarian who was highly valued by horses, his clients, and his friends. I believe that the fates of Pennylane and Johannes were linked, though I do not know in what way. Perhaps they met each other again. Perhaps her spirit welcomed Johannes after his death.

One of the cases that has touched me deeply concerns the horse Hockey. We were in a stable owned by Michel Robert, a great French rider. I was accompanied by the horse dentist Ludovic and by Catherine from Rixheim. The evening before, I had an intuitive flash that Ludovic needed to be present and that I would know why once I arrived at the stable.

The horses had just entered—returning from a competition far away—and they were leaving the van one by one. In this departure, one of the horses had been injured. A stable boy called over the horse's rider and told him they had an emergency situation. The horse was now standing in front of me with blood all over his mouth and pieces of skin hanging here and there. His jaw was broken, the bone split in two so that half of his jaw was hanging loose on one side, and blood was flowing everywhere. I looked at him with dismay. Michel asked for my assistance, while I, for my part, was thinking that we needed a veterinarian. To me, any healing of the horse without medical attention belonged in the realm of the impossible. Yet we were far from the nearest veterinary clinic, so we had to do something. All the people around us were pale and starting to panic.

Michel was counting on me. I started by requesting aid from the Creator, Great Spirit. Through the unexpected miracle of spontaneous inspiration, I knew exactly how to proceed. I remained extremely calm. I knew that Hockey was suffering intense pain, but I also knew that we only had a few hours in which to get the jawbone back into its proper place. The horse's mouth was washed, and I pointed out where Michel and Ludovic should take up their posts. Meanwhile, I continued praying with them, concentrating on my vision of recovery. All three of us had our hands on Hockey's jawbone. A half hour later the jawbone was almost back in its rightful position. We often stopped to wash the horse's mouth again before resuming our work. The three of us were all animated by the same intention, the same idea, and the same desire: we were all completely focused on Hockey's recovery.

We worked for six hours on Hockey, who, despite the pain, understood full well what was happening. With a display of patience, politeness, and a nobility of character, he allowed us to proceed. He knew we were helping him. The junction of the jawbone that had been dislocated went back into place. All of his injuries were treated, one after the other. Last, we gave him grain broth, and late in the night Ludovic went down to the stable again to put antiseptic compresses on the injured area.

The next day Hockey was able to chew hay. Because we could still see a slight gap between his teeth, I asked the Creator what we should do. I learned that Ludovic should file the horse's teeth to adjust them. He worked on Hockey with a great deal of compassion, patience, and application, and the next day the jawbone seemed perfect. I knew that if the jaw remained in place for the next three days, then Hockey would be all right. Three days later, in fact, everything was still in its proper position, and Hockey was eating normally, as if nothing had happened.

I have gone through a number of important events in my life, but it was Hockey who taught me to cast away my doubt. If I am feeling unsure, I need only think of him and all my confidence returns. Similarly, when I think about his noble nature and patience, I can feel etched in my memory the imprint of his radiant personality. The more I grow to know horses, the more I marvel at what they are. A spirit doctor said to me: *Tendras mas como el el cuando tengas confianza* (You will have others like him, if you have confidence).

I was in France and was looking forward to three days of relaxation before my next workshop. During this time I suddenly felt an intense need to visit Blackey, my little donkey, who was calling to me. He had originally come from Romania with many other donkeys. They had been packed together tightly in the back of the same truck, which was to take them to France to be sold. Half of them died en route. Ken and Valerie had rescued several of them, and these were living in a field facing Magali's house.

The first time I had met them at Magali's, one year earlier, I fell in love with two four-month-old brothers: Blackey and Bibou. They were both sweet and innocent, as if unaffected by the tragedy of their journey. I held both of their heads in my hands, and we looked into each other's eyes for a long time. I felt their sweetness fill me. Blackey had a deformed leg. When he was little apparently someone had put it in a splint. During the year after our first meeting I saw him several times. Now I strongly felt I had to rush to see Blackey; it was urgent to help him, whatever the cost.

When I reached Magali's house in the Upper Savoy region, I could see Blackey, still little, although he was now a year older. He was waiting at the back of the field with his head down. He looked scrawny and was tottering as if his legs could barely hold him upright. His coat was filthy, rough, and tangled. The other donkeys had pushed him away and were now ignoring him. He was alone and abandoned. He looked as if he had lost all desire to live. He seemed depressed, as if a massive, thick black cloud surrounded him.

That entire day I stayed close by him. He seemed dehydrated, but the other donkeys would not let him near the water trough; they kept pushing him away. I tried to get him to drink out of the palm of my hand and to get him to eat something. Valerie came to see us. She spoke to Blackey, asking him to keep living, but Blackey just let his head drop down on her knees, as if he was completely exhausted by life. Ken telephoned a veterinarian to ask him to come see him the next day. Magali then joined us after getting home from a long day at work.

We sat down on the grass next to Blackey, trying to get him to drink an improvised saline glucose solution with the aid of a pipette. Night had fallen, and a storm was threatening. My little donkey was lying down and had clearly lost all desire to live, but I was just as adamant that he stay on this earth. I refused to accept the fact that he might die. We had to save him at any price. Magali and I decided to bring him up to the house. We rolled him up in blankets to transport him, and Magali found strength from I know not where: she picked him up in her arms and carried him, but after a few steps, we set him down again because she was exhausted. His eyes became vitreous. We could not even tell if he was still breathing.

We kept starting toward the house, over and over again. Then a moment came when we were both sure he was gone. There was nothing in his eyes anymore. I told Magali: "We should stop here and pray." We lowered onto the wet grass Blackey's heavy and lethargic body, still wrapped in blankets. I put my hands together and asked for help. Little by little I felt a presence entering me. I could observe it, as if it was in the background. This presence looked my little donkey in the eye and spoke to him while flooding him with love—that love we rarely feel among ourselves here on the earth. It is ever-present and infinite, full of compassion and understanding. I felt that this presence was speaking to my little Blackey. It explained the situation to him and offered him a choice.

At this moment it seemed Blackey recovered a bit. We brought him into Magali's house and put him in my room. I stretched out next to him on the floor with my head against his. He made tiny snoring noises, like a newborn. Exhausted, I dozed in the hot breeze of his breath, cradled by this sound. He woke me abruptly in the middle of the night because he tried to stand up. I was scared that he might hurt himself, and I ran upstairs to get Magali. We took him back outside and laid him down on the cool grass. I thought we might have saved him.

Around five o'clock in the morning I could see Blackey outside, standing on his feet and eating grass. Magali had gone down several times during the night to give him the glucose solution through the pipette. He seemed to be doing better. Ken arrived early in the morning and tried to care for him. He spoke to the donkey with great tenderness. I was feeling rather relieved. I was planning to leave soon for Switzerland with Catherine, who had driven from Rixheim to pick me up, because we had a rendezvous with Patrizio. During my trip I could not stop thinking about my little Blackey. He called to me several times after we left. I could see him as if he were right in front of me. I felt that we had to turn around and go right back to give him a perfusion. When we arrived, however, Magali was crying and at the end of her strength. Blackey was lying on the ground, half conscious, his eyes looking glassy again. I was unable to react.

Catherine, who had already grasped the situation, told me: "Ask him if he wishes to remain or leave." I did not think I would be capable of doing it, despite my long experience as a communicator, because my pain was so great. Yet I made the effort: I sat down on the ground and closed my eyes. Blackey instantaneously approached me with a great deal of kindness and charity in his large eyes that glowed with tenderness. "Please, let me go." I came back to my friends who sat around his body. I was blinded by my tears, my throat was choked up, and I was unable to speak. They understood.

The question of euthanasia arose. Blackey asked me to stay with him. The veterinarian was late and would not reach Magali's for two more hours. Magali did not have the strength to witness Blackey's departure. She went into the house, but she was with me in my heart: Blackey had united us forever. The veterinarian gave Blackey a shot and my little donkey left quite peacefully while I held him in my arms. I could not stop crying. Why did he have to leave? Valerie asked me if I wished to remain alone with him. I stayed awhile in silence with his spirit, then I gently covered his body with a blanket.

In the house, Catherine looked at me compassionately and consoled me. She spoke to me about the passage of the spirit, and she was right, but my grief was too great. I could feel only that Blackey had created an indestructible bond between Magali and me. That night I was unable to sleep. All of a sudden, though, a clear, light presence came to lie down next to me. It was my little donkey, now clean and soft as down, looking at me with large, luminous eyes. I wrapped my arms around his neck and dozed with him in the deep peace of his aromatic breath. When I woke again at dawn, the little donkey was gone, but in his place I heard a very delicate voice: "Love everyone, love others, love the All." Simultaneously I felt a powerful sensation of an immense love for everyone. It seemed to me that I had new lenses that allowed me to see the reality of each and every individual. Everything was so simple and clear; everything seemed so obvious. I felt as if I had been liberated and was no longer limited by my customary perceptions. I prayed that this would become permanent. If only it could last!

25

❦

Light

Just like oil is in every part of the olive, love permeates the whole of Creation.

SRI YUKTESWAR

One of the spirit doctors tells me, *"Nunca mas vas a estar sola"* (You shall never be alone again). When I was still living in Madrid, a year after the birth of my twins, I fell deathly ill. No one knew why. I could no longer eat. I weighed no more than one hundred pounds. I knew I was dying, but I no longer had the strength to fight to live. I could not even summon the strength to care. I knew only that if I were admitted to a hospital, it would be the end.

It was the middle of July and more than one hundred degrees in the street, yet I was under every blanket in the house and was still shivering from the cold. I had no idea how I was going to get out of this fix, and I did not even have the energy to think about it. At this time a large conference that involved shamans from all over the world was taking place in Madrid. One of these was a man named Yechiel, a kabbalist living in Israel who had come to talk about the kabbalah. Adam, with whom I was living at that time, had been asked to translate Spanish to Hebrew for him, but he responded: "My wife is very weak right now. I do not know if I can leave her alone." Yechiel told him simply: "I am going to do something." I knew nothing of all this.

During the night I woke up feeling an intense heat. I started throwing my covers off one by one because I was so hot. In front of me I felt a large, luminous, extremely tangible presence. It embodied all the colors of the rainbow covered with gold sequins. I felt that this presence was speaking to me, but I heard no words. This light pulled my entire body toward it. I was so hot that it seemed as if heat was sliding into all of my limbs. I felt as though my entire body was breathing. During this period of my life I had been feeling a great deal of anger toward the Creator, because it seemed to me that I was stuck in Madrid with twin babies and that I lived the kind of poverty that artists experienced—but it no longer seemed as romantic as it was portrayed in the fin de siècle nineteenth-century novels. Some days we did not know if we would have enough to eat—and now I was close to dying, but at this particular moment the only thing that mattered was this light.

The next day I was able to get up out of bed and walk. Yechiel told me: "It is only for you that there was this miracle. This never happened for me before, and it will never happen again." He was fully aware that it was his kabbalistic prayers that had healed me. Yechiel died several years later in Israel.

I recently had the opportunity to go back to Israel, and there, in Galilee, I visited the tombs of the great kabbalists: Rabbi Akiba, Rabbi Isaac Luria, and Shimon Bar Yochai. I felt as though I lived in an older era. The sand-colored stones in Safed seemed to vibrate beneath the burning Middle Eastern sun. The white tombs—those of the saints marked with a blue symbol—dazzled my eyes. I was looking to find some kind of understanding here, but no answers came, despite my keen desire. When I stood beneath the Wailing Wall, however, I knew my prayers were always heard.

I never learned to pray when I was growing up. When I was a child in Formentera we were taken to church every weekend, but the priest was always completely drunk, and rumors ran wild about him and the little boys in the village. I tried to dissuade my brother from going anywhere near him. Not only was I afraid of this priest, but I also found him disgusting. In Formentera, then, I did not at all like attending church. All the people of the village, dressed in their Sunday best, crammed themselves inside the church. It was always stifling hot. The women's fans clacked in tune at the end of every sentence the priest uttered. There were always many women dressed all in black who wept in silence and mumbled unintelligible phrases. I never understood a word the priest said, and I never knew when to sit or stand. In addition, I did not like the morbid images of Christ on the cross. I thought that Christ did not look as he was depicted. I knew him in the most secret recesses of my heart—and he was nothing at all like the images of him in church.

Later, the woman who took care of us, Manuela, became a Jehovah's Witness. She had not learned to read as a child so she learned how to read by reading the Bible. She read very slowly, out loud, following along with her finger on each word. There were images of Jesus in her Bible. He looked like an All-American Boy with blond hair and apple cheeks that were cleanly shaved. The publisher of this Bible had removed his beard—probably because a beard was worn by the malos (evildoers), except for my father, who, according to Manuela was the only *bueno* (good person) on the island who wore a beard. In fact, the *malos* were arrested by the *tricornios,** the fascist police. When I was little, despite the end of the Franco era, there were still three tricornios living on the island. They arrested all men wearing beards—unless these men held an American passport. They let my father go immediately. There were many people on the island who talked about the horrors of Franco and his government. When I was a child I wondered if life under Franco was the same as hell.

Manuela terrified us with her descriptions of hell, which, according to her, was where we were all heading. In hell there was fire everywhere, and

*[This refers to the tricorner hats worn by the state militia. —*Trans.*]

the wicked roasted slowly in it, always moaning. Manuela also enjoyed giving us the somber details of what took place when anyone first set foot in hell. It gave me nightmares! Because we were *antiguos* (ancients), she said, we were going to be expelled into Limbo . . . forever. Yet this was still better than going to hell (though it was not very exciting). Manuela removed the large cross under which she used to sleep. This precipitated terrible fights with her husband, Vincente, who remained a staunch Catholic. Every morning I wondered if I would see the cross back in its customary place on the wall. All the bedrooms on the island had a cross over the bed.

When I went to a French school in Paris, I began hearing about catechism. All that I can remember about it is the other children saying: "A black ant, in a black night, on a black stone. God sees him." The teacher tried to instill fear in them to prevent them from misbehaving. If we misbehaved even a bit God would see it and punish us. We came from sin and we would die in sin. Yet this made no sense to me. Why was God so obsessed with a black ant? Why did he have such a strong desire to punish us? This, too, gave me nightmares. I could not stop myself from thinking about the poor black ant.

My parents often brought us to visit the churches in Spain as well as the Prado Museum when we went to visit my aunt, who lived in Madrid. I loved the light captured in the paintings by El Greco. Here, in these paintings, all was veritable and true: the expressions on the faces, the Holy Ghost like a dove between the people and the sky. My parents wanted to educate us without any religion so that we could form our own opinions. They often talked to us about history. My mother knew the Bible well and regarded it from a historical point of view. She had also learned yoga in Los Angeles, and we owned a copy of the book *Autobiography of a Yogi*. I spent hours looking at the photo of Paramahansa Yogananda on the cover and drinking my fill of the love emanating from his eyes. It was as if he was looking at me and watching me grow up while waiting for me. I knew that he was waiting for me. The honey of his eyes was waiting for me.

When I was young my father initiated me into the reading of the mystics and philosophers of the East. He suggested I read specialized works of Gurdjieff, Ouspensky, Sufism. I devoured everything. I wanted to see, to feel, to understand, to know, to emerge from maya* and pierce the veil of illusion. I was thirsty for knowledge, but I knew that there was still something else to which I had not yet been given access. When I looked at a painting or statue of Jesus Christ, the Virgin Mary, Krishna, or Buddha, I knew that there was something impossible to grasp behind these representations—something I wanted to discover no matter what the cost. They all radiated the same sensibility that I saw emanating from the depths of Yogananda's eyes. What I wanted was not to be found in books, and I did not know how to go about finding it. Yet I continued reading everything that fell within arm's reach.

Several years after my arrival in the United States, I was giving courses in Spanish dance at the University of Pomona, in California. I detested these because the town was far away and I had to take the highway to get there, and I did not know how to drive. In addition, the job did not pay well, and it was obvious that the students did not care at all about the art of flamenco.

Every time I went there I felt I was entering the distant, alien America, but I also was drawn to return because of the horses in a large field that formed part of the university campus. These purebred Arabian horses were there because of the agriculture department, which was an important part of the university. Every Wednesday, carrying a bag of carrots and apples and my dance shoes, I went to see them. They were delighted to partake of these offerings and were grateful to me, but once the bag was empty, they would all leave—except for one.

He was a magnificent dappled white horse. He remained close to me, despite the fence, and enveloped me with his presence and his aroma. I felt joyful when I was with him. It was as if the course and the university ceased to exist. The Mexican student who accompanied me spoke

---

*Maya is one of the terms given to *illusion* in the philosophy of India.

very rapidly, but in the horse's presence I stopped listening to her. Her voice became a flood of words taking place outside my world. I thought of my purebred all week and waited impatiently for Wednesday. The moment the horse spotted the car he came galloping over, and when I parted from him reluctantly to teach my course, he stationed himself in the back part of the field and watched the car as it receded into the distance. I felt as if a rope connected my heart to his, and this rope was stretched every time I left his presence.

One day when I stood in front of him after giving him two apples, I saw in a flash a dazzling light in his eyes. It was stunningly brilliant, and at the same time I felt a great rending in my heart. This light entered me with such force that it took my breath away. All around me the world went dark. It was as if there was nothing—no more world, no more reality. There were only our two minds inside this whirlwind of intense light.

I no longer even seemed to be breathing, I did not even know if I existed, because there were no more bodies, no more me and him—there was just incredible light. Eventually, when I came back to the world, my student companion was still talking a mile a minute, but I was no longer the same. All my cells recalled this recent sensation, and they were vibrating at top speed.

Some time later, on a Wednesday, I made my way to the field as usual, but he was no longer there. I looked for the horse everywhere—in all the neighboring fields. No one could tell me what had become of him. I handed in my notice a short while later and have never gone back. The light was gone.

When I lived in Temple City, a Los Angeles neighborhood that is now primarily Chinese, I tried to practice meditation every morning. Despite the name of this city, it had no temples. I supposed we should find the temples within. While I meditated my little rabbit, Jasmine, who lived in the dance studio, chewed on my toes. This was her morning ritual.

One morning I felt a dazzling presence that filled the entire room.

It was like an airy white wave made of luminous cotton that filled all of us—Jasmine, the room, and me. This presence was absolute peace and serenity. I felt so much love inside me and around me that it was as if all time had paused. I no longer moved, I no longer breathed. I seemed nailed to my chair.

Jasmine had also stopped wrinkling her nose and had started listening. I knew that this was something immense. After a long moment the presence left, but the density of the air in the room remained unchanged for another three days. Everything appeared luminous and alive. I could feel this light every time I entered the room. After this experience I began practicing meditation with fierce determination every morning in hopes of repeating these sensations, but nothing came of it. I grew discouraged and stopped meditating for several years. The only trace of this event: every time I picked up Jasmine in my arms, my hands became burning hot, and I felt a delicate sensation of a white, luminous breath around my head. Every time, Jasmine rolled over onto her back, exposing her soft and vulnerable belly, her little paws up in the air, her eyes half closed, her nose turned up, and her mouth open, showing her white front teeth. We both remained in this state of total quiet, rediscovering what we had once experienced together.

After about twenty minutes the sensation evaporated. Jasmine rolled over, her dark eyes wide with surprise and her little nose quivering. She leaped down from my arms and hopped over the floor of my studio. This happened until I had the experience with the wolf in Yellowstone. During this same period I moved into a new house so that I could live in the San Fernando Valley. My beloved little Jasmine died on one of the first days following the move—almost right on the heels of my return from Yellowstone, where I had my encounter with the wolf.

Ever since my meeting with the wolf I have been fortunate enough to receive wonderful experiences. I have also gone through several stages of extremely painful dark nights, during which I felt completely alone and abandoned, without any support and without any meaning to my life.

No estas sola. No te abandones tu (You are not alone; it is you who are abandoning yourself), one of the spirit doctors told me. I wondered what that could mean. By virtue of abandoning myself I had realized many things with both my head and my heart. If I was able to melt into the interior of another being, slip into his emotions, blow into his tears, float in his body, it is because we are interchangeable. We are all children of the Creator and connected to each other—all of us joined to the Great All. The other and the self I know as me are one and the same.

Animals, meanwhile, look at us without judgment and without condemnation. They feel who we truly are. Through animals we learn how to look this same way at ourselves and those close to us—whether animals or human beings. If we judge someone, we should ask ourselves how the Creator looks at this person. It is this way of looking that I must cultivate within myself until it becomes permanent.

I have also realized, thanks to communication, that everything is a mirror of our beliefs and our way of perceiving the world. Animals are the preeminent mirrors. Through their behavior and their health, animals show us who we really are in our lives and what may be our true thoughts and emotions. Animals reflect our mind and spirit. Through our animal companions we are able to know ourselves better, which allows us to bring about our profound transformation.

In realizing that animals reflect who we truly are, I also have come to understand that our perception of reality reflects our identity, what we are thinking as well as our states of mind. Yet it is not only animals who listen to us. The Great All also listens and speaks to us. All our thoughts, all our emotions are heard and sent back to us through our experiences.

I have observed that there is a direct correlation between my work, the healing treatments, and my state of mind. When I am going through a dark night everything comes to a complete halt from one day to the next; everything stagnates. There is no help in being active; it is as if everything is on hold and waiting. Once I reconnect again, everything rushes back triumphantly—the animals recover, and there is a very clear sensation of joy in the air. The more this happens, the more obvious it becomes to me. I have noticed that if I am sad, depressed, or negative, if I am critical, then everything comes to a screeching halt. I perceive an empty world in which I feel abandoned. When this is my starting point, everything turns out poorly and follows in sequence from there. Problems pile up, matters of concern grow larger, insignificant but irritating circumstances or situations keep showing me insistently the state I am in.

When everything is off kilter in this way, e-mails vanish in the computer as if swallowed by a black hole, the mailman shows up with the package I've been waiting for and I am still in the shower, clients cancel, I get the time wrong, I arrive late, the train pulls out just as I reach the station, letters get lost, and so forth. In short, everything is topsy-turvy, unorganized, chaotic. I feel more and more divided.

Once I realize what is going on, however, I quickly have to change my frame of mind. After making this inner change everything falls back into place and my world becomes clear and favorable. All is synchronized, I meet the people I must meet, I am at the right place at the right time, everything is in harmony. It is up to me to pay attention to what I am broadcasting with my thoughts and sense. A spirit doctor tells me: *Si estas bien dentro de ti, todo se armoniza contigo* (If you are doing well on the inside, everything will come into harmony with you).

The spirit doctor also tells me: *Si buscas encuentras. Recibiras todo lo que deseas. Las cosas no vienen ni antes ni después* (Seek and you shall find; everything you truly desire shall be given to you. Events arrive neither before nor after, but at the right time). He has repeated this to me many times—but it always leaves me confused. I no longer know how to distinguish between fate and free will.

He answers: *El sol siempre sube y se pone el mismo lugar. No lo puedes cambiar. Puedes gritar, llorar y patalear, el sol siempre se levantara al mismo lugar. Lo que si, te puedes levantar mas temprano para ver el sol al alba* (The sun always rises and sets in the same place. There is nothing you can do to change that. You can yell, cry, and stamp your foot, but the sun will always rise in the same spot. The only thing you can do is get up earlier to see the sun rise). I still find much to think about in these words.

This is a story from the time when the human people still knew how to talk with animals.

A Cheyenne hunter returned from the hunt with the meat from a stag he had killed wrapped in the animal's hide. This was during a period of famine, and even though the stag was not enough to feed the entire tribe, he was still happy to be going back with some food. On the return route back to his village he heard a magnificent song that he had never heard before. He realized quickly that it was a song in Cheyenne. He headed toward the voice and came upon a small valley in which he saw a she-wolf with her pups next to their den. They were all sick and scrawny, because they had not eaten for a long time. All the animals were weak and needed food if they were to survive. The hunter grasped the situation quickly, and without hesitation he cut off a piece of the meat and offered it to the she-wolf. She ate a small portion then gave the rest to her pups. The hunter resumed his journey, happy about his gesture, even though he had less food to bring back to his village.

That very night the young man saw in a dream a magnificent woman with long dark hair clad in a robe of white hide with long fringes. She spoke to him: "Today you saved my children and me thanks to the food you gave us. We are all connected in the same sacred circle of life that you had the wisdom to respect today with your generosity. For this reason I am going to give you the song of the spirit of the wolf, and if you sing it to the spirits of the four directions when you are hunting, you will always find good food for your family. Listen to it closely now and remember it."

The words of the song say, "we know the traditional way," which means that we know that we can ask and receive aid from the Creator and that we are connected with the Creator as well as all living things.

I thank the Creator for having given me this life; for having placed in it all those I love, both animal and human; for the doctors of heaven; and for having allowed me to glimpse an infinitesimal portion of the radiance of his love.

Index

abandonment, fears of
  Fay's story, 24–25
  and illness, 182–83
  messages from the spirit doctors, 198, 199
  Sunny, the greyhound, 26–28
abuse of animals
  Bello the racehorse, 182–83
  Ebony's story, 39–40
  Gladys and Spring, 139–40
  horses, 96–97
  how to heal, 54–55
  Promise's story, 52–54
adoption of animals, 34–35
afterlife of animals
  and bringing joy during life, 172–73
  the choice to leave life, 173–74
  Djeda's story, 176–77
  the Hungarian bay horse, 175–76
  messages from, Frank's story, 177–78
  Miguel's story, 49–50
  Soleil's story, 142–44
Amma (Mata Amritanandamayi Devi), 1, 95

Anandamurti (Sri), 109
animal communication. *See* communication with animals; *specific animals*
artists, the critical nature of, 14
Azagra, Rodrigo de, 102

babies and animals, 26–28
Bhagavad Gita, 172
birds
  Brutus, the parrot, 156–57
  as messengers, 79–85
  Snow, the cockatoo, 40–43
bones, fractures of, ix, 71, 74
boredom in animals
  as cause of disease, 43
  Daisy's story, 169–70
  and depression, 10, 40
  and leaving their guardians, 160
Buddha, 89, 167, 168

"capturing"
  an animal presence, 16–17
  what lies behind words, 87

caretakers of animals. *See* guardianship of animals

cats
bringing joy, 172–73
cat gurus, 120–26
chocolate poisoning, 60–61
Chulo, the author's cat, 47–48, 106–7
diabetes, Missy's story, 57
epilepsy, Negrito's healing, 64–65
fighting, Rosie's story, 29–30
Gatulina's story, 108–11
illnesses as communications, 129–30
Princess' thirst, 57–58
protecting their guardians, 152
stress, absorbing, 75–76
centering ourselves
and the process of communication, 73–75
to see through an animal's eyes 17-18
Chateaubriand, François René de, 120
Cheyenne legends, 105–6, 200–201
chi, 102
children and animals
babies in the home, 26–28
teaching them kindness to animals, 32–33
chocolate, as poison, 60
communication with animals
about traveling, 23–24
after their death, 174–75
birds as messengers, 79–85
concreteness of, xiv
the desire to help them, 63
explanation of, 14–20
lessons learned from, 112–13, 198
as mastered by animals, 19
patience, necessity of, 55, 56
process of, 15–20, 72–74
reflections to guardians, 111–19, 130
simple communications, 21–33
for their safety, 15
their wish to communicate, xiv
tuning in, 16–17
communicators
responsibilities of, xiii–xiv
training and the desire to help, 70
competitions for animals
Brendan's story, 25–26
evaluating horses for, 35–36
Lady and Noemi's story, 28–29
Leonard's colic, 68
consciousness of everything, 18
coyotes, 15, 159–60, 167–68
Creator, the
as the healer, 180
oneness with all beings, 198, 201
questions to, 72–74
as source of communication to animals, xiii–xiv
Crowfoot (Blackfoot Warrior), 145
cruelty to animals. *See* abuse of animals

death of animals
animals' response death of their companions, 43
Blackey, the donkey, 186–90
Chulo, the author's cat, 47–48
Duchess' story, 170–71
and forgiveness, 142–44
healing and passing on, 183–84
and letting go, 20, 129

a lost cat, 159–60
Popi's story, 70
putting them down, 184–85
a rabbit, 168–69
surviving for their guardians, 138
Tsareina's story, 51–52. *See also*
    afterlife of animals; euthanasia
death of guardians
    Johannes, 184–85
    Sunshine's story, 80–81
del Monte, Laila
    beginning healing work, 100–104
    career as a dancer, 13–14
    childhood on Formentera, 7–12,
        132–34, 168–69, 192–93
    childhood religious training, 192–95
    Gatulina's story, 108–11
    with the Gypsies, 86–88
    healed by the doctors of heaven, 91–94
    illness in Madrid, 191–92
    with Jasmine, her rabbit, 196–97
    lessons from her dogs, 145–49
    path as a healer, 180–82
    signs to help horses, 95–96, 99–100
    wolf, meeting a, 5–6
depression in animals
    and boredom, 40
    as cause of disease, 43
    Miguel the goat's story, 49–50
    Tsareina's story, 51–52
desires of animals, 15, 97
desire to live
    Bello, the chestnut horse, 182–83
    Blackey, the author's donkey, 187–90
    Daisy's story, 169–70
    Miles' story, 61–62

Shelbi and Rom, 129
Sunny's story, 26–28
Tremendo's story, 50–51
and unconditional love, 54
disease in animals. *See* illnesses of
    animals
doctors of heaven, 91–95
dogs
    Audrey, the go-between, 117–18
    the author's dogs, 101–2, 145–49,
        179–80
    and babies, 26–28
    behavior problems, 114–16
    breeding problems, 130
    cancer, 63–64, 139–40
    caregivers, adopting a new one, 107–8
    children and puppies, 31–33
    and competitions, 25–26
    Daisy's story, 169–70
    epileptic fits, 141–42
    fear of abandonment, 24–25
    fear of daylight, 76–77
    forgiveness, Max's story, 135–36
    guardians, caring for, 150–52, 171
    guardians, protecting, 113–14,
        150–52
    happiness of, 22–23
    illnesses, absorbing, 137
    illnesses as communications, 128–29
    love, the need for, 152–53
    Popi's death, 69–70
    putting to sleep, 170–71, 173–74
    Scooter's story, 68–69
    self-respect, the lesson of, 153–54
    separation anxiety, 157–58
    Tatonka's eye surgery, 62–63

Toby's healing and passing, 183–84
training of, 28–29
Tsareina's story, 51–52
donkeys
Ara's story, 133
Blackey's story, 186–90
doubt, as enemy, 102

Eagle Chief (Letakos-Lesa), 13
egoic involvement in animal
    communication
feelings of superiority, xiv
leaving behind, 63
elk, communication with, 2–3
emotions
absorbed by animals, xiii
exploration of, with animals, 20
similarities of all species, 33
euthanasia
Blackey's story, 189–90
Geboy's story, 173–74

fear in animals
Merlin the horse, 158–60
of separation from a mate, 44–47
of surgery, 62
Tsareina's story, 51–52
feelings of animals. *See* emotions
fighting amongst animals, 29–30
flamenco dance, 86–88, 91–94
forgiveness, lessons from animals, 135–
    39, 141–44
Formentera, author's childhood on,
    7–12, 132–34, 168, 192–93
Francis of Assisi, 127
freedom of animals, 19–20, 164, 166

Gandhi (Mahatma), 136
glaucoma, Tatonka's story, 62–63
goats, Miguel and his horse, 49–50
God, childhood ideas of, 194
Great Spirit. *See* Creator
grief in animals
Miguel the goat's story, 49–50
Noche's story, 47–48
guard dogs, 145–46
guardianship of animals
absorbing stress, 75–76, 127
Charm's story, 30–31
freedom, acknowledging animals',
    19–20, 166
help, asking for, 136–37
illnesses, recognizing, 68
loyalty of animals, 80–81
receiving communications,
    112–13
reflections of the inner states of,
    111–19, 120–26, 127–28
selling a horse, 54–55
Snow's story, 40–43
guarding the guardian. *See* protection
    of the guardian
Gypsies, 86–88, 181–82

happiness of animals
George the bulldog, 22–23
and healing, 65
Toby's story, 183–84
Tommy the poodle, 108
worms, 71
healing of animals
experiences of, 65, 100–104,
    179–80, 182, 185–86

and letting go, 69–70, 186–90

Miles' story, 61–62

helping animals

  can be learned, 67

  and the desire to communicate with, 63, 70

  and state of mind, 198–99

herbs for animals, 75

Hicks, Jerry and Esther, 79

Hippocrates, 56

horses

  and the afterlife, 175–78

  anxiety about being sold, 37–39, 164–65

  anxiety about profitability, 54–55

  Aube's pregnancy, 70

  balance problems, 67

  Bello the racehorse, 182–83

  boredom in, 43

  caretakers, 30–31

  character of, 40

  control over their lives, their lack of, 165–66

  cruelty to, the results of, 38–39, 96

  emotional work with, 77–78

  evaluation of, for competition, 35–36

  feelings of, sensitivity to, 43–47

  forgiveness, lessons in, 139

  guardians, reflections to, 111–12, 113, 130–32

  the healing of Hockey, 185–86

  Kia's healing, 58–60

  Lyme disease, 61–62

  nervousness, 74–75

  Patrizio's work with, 97–98

  Promise's healing, 52–54

putting down, 184–85

riding positions for comfort, 37

Tremendo, and the joy of living, 50–51

hysteria, Fay's story, 24–25

iguanas, Freddy's story, 21–22

illnesses of animals

  Argenon's tumor, 136–37

  arthritis, 182–84

  Aube's pregnancy, 70–71

  boredom as a cause of, 43

  cancer, 63–64, 137–38, 142–44

  chocolate ingestion, 60–61

  daylight, fear of, 76–77

  epilepsy, healing of, 64–65

  expressing the states of their guardians, 128–31

  glaucoma, Tatonka's story, 62–63

  Kia's story, 58–60

  Lyme disease, 61–62

  Missy's diabetes, 57

  poisoning, 66–67

  Princess' story, 57–58

illnesses of guardians

  Beau's story, 63–64

  Garnet's care of Petra, 129–30

  Shelbi's depression, 129–30

injuries, sensitivity to, 37–38

interspecies communication. *See* communication with animals

Jung, Carl, 86

kabbalists, 192

Kabir, 150

lessons taught by animals, 145–49

leukemia, 71

listening to animals

author's lesson of, 44–47

Daisy's story, 169–70

and the Great All, 198

to horses, to help riders, 37–40

importance of, 17, 75–76, 79

and people, 113, 130–31

process of, 73–74, 86–87

loneliness and animals, 139, 169

lost animals

Freddy the iguana, 21–22

receiving images and sensations from, 16

Tommy the poodle, 107–8

what they contend with, 159–60

love

animals helping their guardians, 63–64, 135–39

in communication with animals, 73–74

as given by animals, 150–52, 154–55

healing trauma and abuse, 54–55

the need for, 152–53

loyalty, 47, 150

Lyme disease, Miles' story, 61–62

Maharshi, Sri Ramana, 34

Mata Amritanandamayi Devi (Amma), 1, 95

messages to animals. *See* communication with animals

mind, state of, 198–99

Mother Teresa, 156

nervousness

Fay's story, 24–25

a horse's desires, 36

and pain, Kia's story, 59–60

Sunny's story, 26–28

Trooper's story, 74–75

ownership of animals, the impossibility of, 19–20. *See also* guardianship of animals

patience

of horses, 97

necessity of, in order to communicate, 56

with traumatized animals, 54, 55

permission to help, asking for, 63, 70

Perry, Ted, 7

personality of animals, 16

photographs, use in animal communication and healing, 16

physical feelings of animals

communication of, 56

Kia's story, 58–60

Missy's story, 57

poisoning, Beauty's story, 66–67

practicing communication with animals, 74

prayer, 74, 192

profitability in horses, their anxiety about, 54–55

protection of the guardian

Alba's story, 145–46

Chloe's story, 113–14

Duncan the cat, 152

Grace's story, 150–52

questions, asking animals, 73. *See also* communication with animals

rabbits
    the author's, 147–48, 168, 196–97
    Mosy's story, 29–30
rejuvenation, Scooter's story, 68–69
riding positions on horses, 37–40

safety of animals, 15
Schucman, Helen, 179
selling of horses
    anxiety and fear of, 54–55, 164–65
    painful results of, 37–39
senses used in animal communication, 15–16
sensitivity to animals' pain, 31–32
separation from other animals
    depression and anxiety due to, 43
    sorrow, 48
    two horses' story, 44–47
separation from their guardians
    acceptance of, 162–63
    anxiety about, 157–58
    Tremendo's story, 50–51
sorrow in animals
    Noche and Chulo's story, 47–48
    for their guardians, 62, 141–42
    Tremendo's story, 50–51
spirits of animals, 179–80
suffering of animals
    in the death of a companion, 48
    in separation from a mate, 47
    See also abuse of animals
symptoms, physical, of animals
    chocolate ingestion, 60–61

communication of, 56
    disguise of, to protect their guardians, 69–70
    Kia's story, 58–60
    Missy's story, 57

teachers, animals as
    cat gurus, 120–26
    Gatulina's story, 109–11
telepathy, in animal communication, 13, 14–20, 86–88
tortoises, Samson's story, 89–90, 100
traumatized animals
    from an earthquake, 78
    author's work in a rescue shelter, 169
    and fear, 156
    horses, selling them, 38, 39–40
    how to heal, 54–55
    from past difficulties, 34
    Promise's story, 52–54
traveling, messages to animals about, 23–24
truth, speaking up for animals, 44
turtles, Tito's story, 126

urination
    as behavioral sign, 120–26
    Daisy's story, 169–70
    and the need for self-respect, 153–54

veterinarians and animal communication, 67–68, 127–28, 184–85
Vianney, Jean-Baptiste-Marie, 162

weaving in horses, 77–78

wolves

    Beauty's story, 66–67

    Cheyenne legends of, 105–6, 200–201

    communication with, 1–6, 197

worms, 71

Yellowstone National Park, 1–2

Yogananda (Paramahansa), 99, 194

Yukteswar (Sri), 191

Ywahoo, Dhyani, 72, 104

Zhou, Master, 102–3

BOOKS OF RELATED INTEREST

Animal Voices, Animal Guides
Discover Your Deeper Self through Communication with Animals
by Dawn Baumann Brunke

Shapeshifting with Our Animal Companions
Connecting with the Spiritual Awareness of All Life
by Dawn Baumann Brunke

Power Animal Meditations
Shamanic Journeys with Your Spirit Allies
by Nicki Scully

Animal Voices
Telepathic Communication in the Web of Life
by Dawn Baumann Brunke

How Animals Talk
And Other Pleasant Studies of Birds and Beasts
by William J. Long

**How to Read the Aura and Practice Psychometry,
Telepathy, and Clairvoyance**
by W. E. Butler

The Chakras in Shamanic Practice
Eight Stages of Healing and Transformation
by Susan J. Wright

Morphic Resonance
The Nature of Formative Causation
by Rupert Sheldrake

INNER TRADITIONS • BEAR & COMPANY
P.O. Box 388
Rochester, VT 05767
1-800-246-8648
www.InnerTraditions.com

Or contact your local bookseller